The Internal Light

Finding Peace in a World Full of Chaos

C.A. Clement

****

Book Cover Design: Marlon J. Mack

*This book is dedicated to my Queen mother
Sheila, aka Monica, aka Superwoman. Your Strength, Light
and unwavering Love over the years has helped me
to find my own voice. Thank you.*

Table of Contents

Introduction

There is an old Hindu legend that tells the story of when all human beings were gods. The story goes that they abused their divinity so much that Brahma, the chief god, decided to take it away from them and hide it where it could never be found.

But Brahma had no idea where to hide it, so he called on the other gods to help him. "Let's bury it deep in the earth," said the gods. "No, because humans will dig into the earth and find it," he replied. Then the gods said, "Let's sink it in the deepest ocean." But Brahma shook his head. "No, they will just learn to dive deeper in the ocean and they will find it." Then the gods said, "Let's take it to the top of the highest mountain and hide it there." Once again, Brahma disagreed, "That will not do either, because they will eventually climb every mountain and once again find their divinity." The gods gave up and said, "We do not know where to hide it. It seems that there is no place on earth that human beings will not eventually reach."

Brahma thought for a while and said, "Here is what we'll do. We will hide their divinity deep in the center of their own being, for humans will never think to look for it there." And there, according to the tale, is where it has been hiding ever since.

In life, it seems as if we are constantly searching for answers in the world. Some profound, great, elusive answer for real, true happiness. And humans are so amazing and resourceful, they will go to great lengths to search, study and explore any and everything within their reach. But sometimes, if we'd just take the time to look deep enough within ourselves, we would find that the answers we need already reside within the depths of our being. We just need to know where to look for them.

Having a good life in many ways can be attributed to two things: living your most complete life with purpose, gratefulness and no apologies, and seizing your moments. Some of these moments you experience in your life affect you in ways you never expected or prepared for... They warm you, they change your heart, they hurt you beyond understanding and they bring you immeasurable joy. As an adult, you've already had many of these moments – they quickly come to mind if you reach for them – and whether they were good or bad, these are the moments that hold the most weight in your life because they've helped to mold the person that you've become.

My hope is that while you read this book, you have a moment. A moment that brings you clarity. Warmth. Encouragement. Courage. And Faith... A moment that helps you see that the light you are looking for, through all the darkness and chaos in this world, was in you all along.

I never thought that the first person this book would help would be me. But as I was writing it, it was a constant reminder that for most of life's issues and confusion, we indeed already have the answers, as well as the light we're constantly searching for, inside of us. It can just feel difficult to reach because it's often clouded by our emotions, experiences, fears, and the constant battle of what we want, versus what we really need. Even when we do know the right answers, we tend to need a reminder every now and then. Writing this book gave me the clarity to stay focused on my own journey in life, to be the example that I am teaching, and to always remember that my happiness is my own, and therefore must come from me.

As you read, understand that whatever it is you want to go after in your life, no matter how difficult or unlikely it may seem, happiness is not only in achieving it, but also in the journey. Stop to look around you and see what you've already accomplished, and feel good about who you are right at this moment. All we have is now, so cherish it. Don't wait for something amazing to happen to find your happiness. YOU are the amazing. Learn to fall in love with yourself. Find your happiness in the life you possess right now. If you truly can't do that, then make the decision to rid yourself of whatever is stealing your smile once and for all, because your internal peace is the most important thing you can possess.

Every human being has the desire for their soul to be happy, to have a mental understanding of all things that matter, and to be at peace. No matter how you go about finding this happiness, this is always the goal. But in the world we live in, everyday problems invade that peace daily. We cannot control the world. We cannot predict the future, nor can we stop the rain when it falls on us. But the one thing we can control is ourselves. We can control how we deal with that rain, with the storms ahead, and with the chaos around us. Once we learn how to see things in a new light, we can start our own journey to seek our inner peace. And once we've found that, then we have truly arrived.

Each experience in your life is a seed. You can disregard that seed and let nothing come of it, or you can hold on to it and allow it grow into something meaningful. You may not always be able to choose your circumstance, but you can always choose how you react to it. This choice is always yours, no matter what it is.

Mahatma Gandhi defined 'Namaste' by saying, "I honor the place within you where the entire Universe resides; I honor the place within you of love, of light, of truth, [and] of peace; I honor the place within you, where, when you are in that place in you, and I am in that place in me, there is only one of us [we are one]."

Therefore, I say to you, *Namaste*. You deserve to be happy. You deserve to find love in your life, as well as within yourself; despite your mistakes, hard times, or any other hurdles that you may have encountered. You have survived them, and you are still here. Hold on and know that even though it may be too late to change some things in your life, every day you are alive is another chance to do something better, to get something right, and to find your own inner peace.

Claim Your Happy.

Real Happiness.

In this world, it's pretty safe to say that everyone wants to live his or her life in a state of happiness. I say "state of happiness" because we'd like to believe that everyone feels happy at some point or another in their lives, even if only for a short while. But when we think of being happy, the true goal is to achieve that state of living where we feel joy or content all or most of the time; and unhappiness or being unsatisfied are feelings that are short-lived, instead of part of our daily lives.

But for happiness to be something that is so sought after, few of us really evaluate what being truly happy even means. We are convinced that once we attain that "one thing" we are presently desiring, we will be happy – whether it be money, love, fame, even marriage or something else entirely. The measure of success – "making it" or "true happiness" – is different for everyone. But is that really what happiness is?

And how can we sustain that happiness over time?

Seems like a strange question to ask. You of all people should know what can or will make you happy, right? But in reality, that isn't always true. The one constant truth amongst most human beings is once you reach an age of awareness, you tend to have a desire for something more. A yearning for more than what you presently have or own. Once you attain this thing you've been wanting, it feels good – even great.

But after time, you realize that the happiness you attained from this achievement is short-lived, and you find yourself once again chasing after something, convincing yourself that once you get this new thing, then you'll really be happy. The problem with this thinking is we are confusing our internal happiness with improving the external quality of our lives. Many people believe that complete happiness will appear once we obtain a lot of money, have someone to love, may-be lose a lot of weight, get recognition for something, etc. – basically anything that you may be chasing at the time.

Desires and goals have a valid merit in the world we live in, and achieving this form of success greatly changes your life. But if every wealthy or "successful" person were tru-ly happy, the world would be a different place. Many rich people in the world are still unhappy. What is missing? The problem is no balance. Although desires and goals are val-id, they are only one aspect of satisfaction. If your internal state is not in balance, whether you've succeeded at a new business, finally won that medal or graduated with honors, that feeling of achievement is not enough to encompass your entire state of happiness.

If you live your life in a constant state of waiting until after you achieve or get something to feel happy, then maybe your basis for happiness should be redefined. The truth is, when we chase after our desires, they really aren't what we are chasing. What we are actually chasing is the happiness we think these things will bring us once we get them. But the reason why we seldom get there, or if we do the feeling doesn't seem to last long, is true happiness is not based on what you have or own. It's a state of mind that you simply feel all the time.

Once attained, this feeling already exists when you wake up in the morning, and remains with you while you carry out your day, your week, and your years. It is fueled by knowledge of self, the things you have learned, the gratefulness you feel and the light that lives inside of you. When this type of happiness is achieved in your life, it not only assists you in achieving all your goals and dreams, but everything else that occurs daily borrows light from this happiness. Then you can feel happy when you simply take a walk on the beach. When someone gives you the smallest gift, or writes you a note. When you have a conversation with a loved one, or a good friend. When you close your eyes and empty your mind of everything, and all you are left with is yourself.

This kind of happiness doesn't wait for you to achieve your life's goals. It lives within you throughout your journey, to help you achieve them. And when you do achieve your goals, the feeling is immense, but it is kept in perspective because you understand what is most important in life. Basically achieving happiness starts with achieving inner happiness and peace, and permeates to your external living. When you feel whole internally, life remains full of things to appreciate, and difficult circumstances don't define you, they are simply things you have to get through to get to the next chapter in your journey. This kind of peace is well within your reach, it just may feel impossible after so many years of chaos. The key is to learn how to face your internal thoughts and examine who you are from within, so you can wipe your inner canvas clean and begin to create a new masterpiece.

And right at that moment, we begin our healing.

Many people think seeking internal happiness means not going after your desires or success. This is simply untrue, as one does not cancel out the other; part of internal happiness is knowledge of self and going after your true passions and purpose – once you go after what you are meant to be doing in this life, success is sure to follow. It must. It is simply the law of how energy and the universe work. If you concentrate on what really matters in your life, all the rest of your wants and needs will come into fruition.

The issue comes in when your pursuits are out of sync. For example, if you only concentrate on making money and neglect what matters in your life, either money will always feel like it's evading you, or you will never make enough money to feel satisfied. But if you concentrate on achieving your purpose and passion, something you were meant to do or be, or what you're meant to teach or share with the world, the money will always come. If you concentrate on finding someone to love you, it will feel like you'll always be alone. But if you learn to love yourself and have unselfish love for others, the love you're looking for will come as if it were always there.

Life is far from easy, but your perspective on it and yourself is everything. Once you realize what is truly important in your life, change your priorities and learn what you should be pursuing to find your sunrise, there will only be light in your horizon, and it will radiate through everything in your path. Your life will not be clouded with confusion or bad choices, and you will not be consumed by the things you've spent so much of your life chasing. They will either come to you willingly, or you will realize that you never needed them in the first place. Then you can truly find happiness in a world full of chaos.

The Internal Light

Explore Within.

So, where do we begin? Before action, we must first gain true understanding,

Many people wonder why happiness always seems to evade them, but don't actually take any steps to change their situation. They believe either you're happy or you're not, as if some people are simply destined for happiness, while others are just not meant to be that fortunate. But being happy is very much a conscious decision. It is not something that just happens. It has nothing to do with how much money you were born into or your status in the world; if you're single or in love; if you're famous or successful in business. Happiness begins, and ends, with the state of your mind, heart and spirit. Therefore, when seeking happiness, we must be aware that it isn't anyone else's job to give us our peace or make us happy. Our happiness is ours to attain, and ours to keep alive and thriving.

In this conscious thinking, we must also know that there is no "quick fix" solution. People often have this idea that if only this "one thing" could happen for them, whatever that 'one thing' is for that person (a relationship, money, success, etc.), then that will make them happy, and everything else will either work itself out on its own, or no longer matter. This thinking would suggest that people would never have to work on themselves within, because after they get this one thing they wanted, everything will magically be all right. Unfortunately, this is simply not true. Winning the lottery, for example, may seem like something that will bring you complete happiness, as many believe that all their problems can be solved with money. But after time has passed and you become used to your new lifestyle, you'll soon realize that not only is this feeling of happiness fleeting, but your new situation also brings with it a new set of problems.

Winning the lottery is great, but it doesn't make you feel successful. It doesn't grant you the respect you yearn for. It doesn't improve your feeling of loneliness, despite more people being around you. In fact, it may even make it worse and bring with it constant trust issues, worrying that people are only befriending you because of your newfound money. And if you were bad with finances before, becoming rich doesn't fix this problem; only now you'll be bad with larger sums of money, and even more credit. This premise is the same with many "quick fix" circumstances. Another example is people thinking a relationship will make them happy and fix all their problems. Being with someone, even a great someone, doesn't improve your feelings of insecurity. It doesn't suddenly make your difficulty to love someone, or your inability to show affection or trust others, disappear. Some women think marriage is the ultimate goal. So they spend a great deal of time working towards getting married, instead of working on the actual union behind the marriage or the person entering into that marriage, so they can stay married for a lifetime.

The fact is being happy doesn't come from a relationship, or becoming rich, or any other quick fix you're thinking of. External things you reach for are meant to complement and enrich your happiness, but it is not the heart of it. If someone wonderful comes into your life, what good is it if you are still broken inside from years of heartbreak, and cannot fully trust or completely love this person? If your life has no purpose and you are not happy within your soul, how can financial success make you feel rich internally, where it counts? If you want happiness in your life, you must stop looking outward and start from within. If you don't fix yourself internally, all that you reach for will be that much more difficult to attain, and will still leave you feeling empty even after you've achieved them. Humans are meant to be fruitful and prosperous. But starting your journey from within provides you with the foundation you need to be internally whole and mentally strong, so that when you do attain your goals, it is that much more fulfilling.

The circumstances in your life right now don't matter. You can make a conscious decision to repair and heal yourself internally despite your present situation. But it will not be easy. Because you will finally have to stop ignoring the things that make you unhappy within yourself, and be choosy with the people you allow into your life. You will have to be willing to face the difficult and uncomfortable situations, like having that conversation you know needs to happen with someone. Or finally walking away from that person you know you should have already left behind. Or facing that truth you've been running from. Or doing that thing for your health that you know needs to be done. Most importantly, you'll have to realize that what you are looking for from others – whether it be love, acceptance, or validity – you must first find within yourself.

Life and circumstances are going to happen whether you decide to be happy or not. Why not make the choice to live the happiest life you can, so you can be in more control of your personal happiness, and your peace?

Many people simply accept whatever circumstance they're in. They feel like no matter what they do, good things will never happen in their life, so they see no point in trying. This type of thinking is common. Sometimes it stems from your environment, fear, complacency, low self-esteem, disappointment, or a host of other things. But before you decide to hold on to that state of mind, follow me in this scenario. Let's say a parent saw someone or something about to hurt their young child. Do you think they would measure their chances of success when trying to protect them? If you were the parent, would you? It's likely that your chances wouldn't matter. The only thing you'd care about is trying with everything you have to get your child out of harm's way. Because at that moment, all you can feel is that you need whatever is happening right now to stop. That feeling overpowers any worries about the consequences of what you're doing, or your chances of success. This scenario may feel extreme, but the premise still stands – whether you succeed or fail is not the reason you fight. You fight because what is taking place right now is not something you are willing to accept, so you do whatever you can in your power to change it. Of course you want to succeed, but even if you don't, not doing anything is far worse than trying with everything you have. And your happiness, your mental and spiritual peace? I'm here to tell you that it is that important. It is that extreme. So fight. Fight through the hard times, fight the fear of the unknown. Fight against the mental slavery of thinking you are less than what you really are, or thinking that you don't deserve more. Fight for your peace, because you are worth it.

People say that they want to be happy, but many of us just live our lives as the day comes, and sit in situations that rob us of our peace. Is it that it doesn't bother us as much as we say it does? I don't think so. Yet we live in it, and allow days, months, even years to go by. We sit in unhealthy relationships. Dead-end jobs. We don't go after our passions. We live unhealthy lifestyles. We don't let go of people or things that we know are no good for us. In other words, we don't nourish our soul, or worse, we stifle our own happiness. And although we say to ourselves we'll fix it "soon," time has no 'slow,' 'pause,' or 'rewind' button. It also has no feelings. So whether you choose to live a meaningful life or not, time is still moving through your life with no apologies, etching memories, writing history and creating experiences as it goes along. These occurrences are things you cannot change once they happen. So the longer you do nothing and merely allow the world to swallow your spirit, the longer time is writing your life story instead of you. And it may not be the story that you want written. You must live in the now, put forth the effort, gain knowledge and exercise will, to elevate your being. Not after you get a better job, or first thing next year. Not after you lose the weight or your significant other gets his/her life together so you could concentrate on you. Not after your kids leave home. You must decide to elevate your quality of life now.

Whatever you're afraid of, the pain will be worth it and the people who leave will not matter, because they weren't supposed to be there in the first place. Failure should never be a reason to not try. When a child first learns to walk, there are many falls. It means nothing more than they are getting closer to succeeding, because with every fall, they learn what not to do. They just keep trying until they succeed. And so it is with everything you learn.

When you begin to seek the life you are meant to be living, you will find that your life will suddenly take you through journey after journey, to get to these amazing goals. During these journeys, you will learn new things, meet new people, and discover things about yourself that you never even knew. You'll become stronger in the face of difficulty, and you will see God's power as the universe puts things and people in your path to help you when you need it the most.

These journeys promote mental, spiritual and emotional growth. Therefore, know that the journey is just as important as the goal. Your life is not on hold until that goal is met. Your life is expanding, growing and improving throughout every step of every journey.

And if you go after what truly matters, wealth of every kind will come to you in abundance.

So what is the definition of happiness and peace? Simply attaining the best life that YOU can live. No one else. Therefore, it cannot come from anyone or anything else. It must be an internal journey that builds outward. Happiness is about being who you are meant to be, going after what's important to you and living a full life. Happiness is having full knowledge of SELF and accepting the person in front of the mirror. Even the bad – you cannot improve what you cannot own. Happiness is being honest about what encompasses your life right now, and finally finding balance. It's recognizing all the good that exists in your life and feeling true gratitude and perspective, while finally accepting if something is not for you and finding the courage to let go, maintaining faith to wait for what is. Happiness is accepting that life doesn't have to be perfect for it to be complete – and knowing this in itself brings forth happiness. A happy life is one that recognizes that each living soul is connected to one another – we therefore must respect and share with one another, teach each other and keep the light shining in all of us. We all have a responsibility to honor that from whence we came, in a way that utilizes the strengths that we now possess because of them. We do this by living a life with constant learning, giving and awakenings. Living a life with the light that exists within you shining brightly, never dimmed. Living a life that feels complete, regardless of what you do or do not physically possess. One that is respectful of other life, and recognizing our deep connection and responsibility to one another. When you find this type of peace and balance, you will find surely find happiness. So make the conscious decision to claim it for yourself. Then set out to go and achieve it.

Know and Love thy Self.

We know that positive change must begin with ourselves. But we cannot fix the things in our life that we haven't even realized needs repairing. Sometimes we are aware of the habits we have and the choices we make, but we don't always know why these things happen to us, or why we even do the things we do. Other times we are not even conscious of things we tend to do over and over. What motivates our experiences? What brought us our fears? What influences our likes? What draws us to one relationship and not the other? What makes us constantly succeed, or continuously miss the mark?

Many people are resistant to the term "knowledge of self," as they believe that when people say you don't have it, what they're really saying is you don't even know yourself. But the meaning of the term goes a little deeper than that. In order to change and improve upon our lives, we must first gain a deep understanding of what makes us do the things we do, and what influences our choices. They are not by chance. Searching for answers within yourself and humbly opening your heart and mind to receive them will cause you to discover things about yourself that you've never known. Things that never dawned on you before. Things that people may have told you in the past, but it never really clicked inside you until now. And whether these things are good or bad, once you are conscious of them, you will feel like a light bulb in your mind has turned on. One that you will never want dimmed. Because suddenly, you'll be able to connect the dots within your life, and things that never made sense to you, now seem very clear. True knowledge of self forms the first real maps that we follow in our journeys through life. Without them, we limit our growth and stunt our potential to be amazing.

When you are willing to uncover the things that affect the decisions you make every day, you'll not only find self-acceptance, the ability to grow and the right tools to heal, but you will also discover your own voice. Life is no longer happening by accident; you know exactly where you're going, and you are at peace with the decisions that you make. Face the opportunities to learn who you are with courage, and when you do, rid yourself of any obstacles that have weighed you down. Only then can you build something up within that is strong, powerful, ever-growing, and always beautiful.

Throughout your life as you grow, you will become more and more enlightened and accepting of yourself, feel more fulfilled and find better perspective. You will also soon learn that you will never stop discovering yourself, because you will never stop growing. But how do you begin this quest for knowledge? Well, you begin like any other search within, you ask yourself questions. Simple questions that every human being should be fully conscious of within themselves. Have you ever known someone who has a personality trait, but is completely unaware of it? Have you ever had more than one person tell you something about yourself that you never truly accepted to be true? Why not? Do you know what your strengths are? Your weaknesses? Do you have personality traits that stem from past experiences? Do you always go after the wrong relationship? When you reach inside yourself to find answers, you create an avenue for you to live your life happily and without apologies.

But learning how to see inward doesn't just come to you. You have to ask yourself questions with an open heart that wants to affect change. Women wonder so often, "Why can't I ever find a good man? What am I doing wrong?" But when they ask these questions, it's usually in a state of depression and pity, and the questions are rhetorical; the person isn't actually looking for the answer. You should look for that answer! This isn't about assigning blame to yourself; it is about grasping the power you need to change your life. We must learn the ability to see inside of us. It can be scary and uncomfortable, but if you face your fears, your insecurities and your mistakes, you can improve upon them. You can then create a new path for your life, instead of continuing to walk in a circle and getting nowhere. And your life deserves better. When you finally look inside of yourself, you'll learn that not only is everything not as bad as you think, but the benefits of knowing exactly who you and living a conscious life with no apologies are is well worth it.

Ask yourself questions that generate the answers you need to affect change. Questioning yourself in a state of pity or pain only breeds more pain. The key is to go back a little further, to a much simpler question. One that screams, "I am ready for change. And I know that change starts with me." For instance, if your problem is: Why is it so hard for me to keep a good job? People tend to ask: *What is wrong with me? Why does everyone else get what they want, but I can never catch a break? Am I just not meant to be successful?* But these are the wrong questions, as no answer to these will be productive to change. Let's go back a little further: *What kind of job do I keep looking for? Is that the right job for me? Do I need to go back to the basics? Is there a common complaint or concern that every job has about me? Is there something I need to address or change?* These are better questions.

Why do I keep getting my heart broken? Am I just not meant to find love? What is wrong with me? Wrong questions. Let's go back a little further: *What kind of person am I attracting, and how am I attracting them? Do I display low self-esteem, or an overly independent attitude? Am I jumping in too fast, before I find out if they're even worthy of my heart in the first place? Should I be looking for someone right now at all? Do I display the same level of qualities as the type of person I'm looking for?* Better questions.

Once you find the answers you are searching for within yourself, your life will take on a new beginning, and just like that, another journey begins.

Once you are fully conscious of who you are, the next step is to own it. Accept all of who you are, not just the person everyone sees. Own your fears and your flaws, because if you don't accept that they exist, you can never fix them. Face your pain so that you can get to the root of it, and conquer it. Accept your past, because you cannot change it. And own your mistakes, because owning them will allow you to never repeat them. If you don't own who you are, then you will be forced to live the same problems over and over again: Same bad relationships. Same bad choices. Same unhealthy lifestyle. Same money problems. Same self-loathing. Same loneliness. No one is dealt a perfect hand in life. But there isn't much that people can't overcome, if you own it.

Your spirit knows your truth, and it will not rest until you're living it. The thought of facing your own demons is scary, but not facing them won't make them disappear. The only thing you'll achieve by running from your truths is giving them power over you. Your state of hiding will then become your weakness. Face your truths, and conquer them. How can you change your path, if you're not honest with yourself about who you are or where you've been? Where you've come from? What your experiences have been? What has been done to you? You cannot change your experiences, but you can face them and get over them. The worst is already over; it happened, and you have survived. It cannot hurt you anymore.

People often stay in hiding because they feel like they are the only ones with regret, or at least the only one in their circle of family and friends. They think they're the only ones struggling. The only ones with uncertainty or fear. They feel like they're the only ones that have been victimized, or even the only ones that aren't as together as they would like to be. Nothing could be further from the truth. If the world were a better place, people would stop hiding, and everyone would see that none of us are as together as we seem, or have done it all right, or are full of insurmountable courage. Maybe then, people wouldn't feel as bad about their shortcomings, or feel so alone in their problems. This shame, fear or guilt of imperfection is something that you haven't earned, because we all are void of perfection.

So here's the truth: none of us have it all together. Not a single adult person you know hasn't done something that they could be consumed with sadness or guilt about, no matter how put together they seem. More people than you will ever know have been treated unfairly, made bad choices, have been in a bad relationship, been victimized in some way, or some other hidden guilt or shame. Some have it together better than others. Some are in a better place at that moment. Some are happier in some areas than others. But we have all struggled with some kind of pain, and no one is fighting through something that someone else hasn't experienced before. There's simply no reason to feel like you are the only person hurting or struggling. Because you far from alone. You are simply a human, trying to get it right and keep going, like the rest of us.

So don't avoid your problems, and don't worry about saving face. Own your mistakes and face your hardships and your pain, so that you can learn from them, conquer them and move forward with your life. If you truly can't find the strength to do that alone, find the courage to take back your life by going out and seeking the help you may need, whether it's advice from a friend or family member, or even help in a professional capacity. It's okay not to have it all together, and it's more than okay to need help – we all do at some point. When you feel afraid to be honest, know that although some people might not be happy with your truths, most will respect you, and more importantly, you can finally respect yourself.

When you've accepted who you are, faced your problems and started working on repairing them, practice living an honest existence, without fear or shame.

Once you have owned the person inside of you, you'll need to accept the physical person standing in the mirror. Whoa... this one can be hard, especially for a woman, the way the world puts so much importance on her outer appearance! But it all depends on how you view it. Take a good look at yourself. Every fold, every feature, every nail and every hair: this is everything that makes up the wonderful being of you. This is your height, and your weight. This is your skin complexion. This is your nose. Everyone in this world wants to be loved... but why should anyone love you if you don't even love yourself? There is only one you, so you have to come to terms with who you are and love that person. Your imperfections are part of your beauty, because they make up who you are. Look at your eyes and see into your soul, and the beauty that lies within it. Look at your hands and your smile. Drink it in. Whatever features you have, remember that as sure as everyone has flaws, it is just as certain that there is someone in the world that will love all of yours. Never forget that. No matter what you look like or don't look like, you are enough. Know that you can never convince someone else you're enough if you don't believe it yourself. But once you accept who you are and appreciate it, others will see your beauty as well.

Confidence is a huge part of what makes someone attractive and beautiful. There is no boilerplate for attractive, no matter what magazines portray. It is simply what someone deems it to be. You may want to improve on some things about yourself and that's okay, but remember to always love the person in front of you right now, no matter what. Because this is you, here and now. And you are all you have.

Being honest with yourself, owning your mistakes, loving who you are and appreciating how far you've come in life, gives you a freedom that nothing or no one else can. The truth is, you can't run from yourself, no matter what you do. So you are either going to live in a world where you are in denial of who you are and always want to be something else – which will never make you happy – or you are going to be a person who knows exactly who you are, exactly where you've come from, and exactly where you want to go. That is strength in itself that once you know it, you'll never want to let go.

Your Internal Light.

A good life has to encompass balance. There are many factors of your life that make up your existence, but what is fundamental to your peace is your internal light.

Let's discuss the three elements that make up this elevated state of living.

Your mind is essential to achieving anything. Every single thing you do and succeed at begins with your mind, and then the body follows. The mind is logical. It contains maps and solutions based on reasoning, learned lessons and experiences that guide you along the way. This reasoning helps you avoid bad outcomes and risky situations. The mind is also ever growing. If it gathers new information, it has no problem changing its present course. The mind is indeed filled with a great deal of valuable information, but the down side is so many options are filled with just as many outcomes, and all this information can make the mind feel confusion or fear. The mind may have the information it needs, but the information only tell you the different avenues or options you can choose from. Without feeling or intuition, your mind can be unsure of what decision is best, or even which result you want to live with in the first place. In the middle of confusion, the mind can take a backseat to depression, stagnation, or impulsive moves.

The mind is your map, but **the heart** is your engine. It is full of feelings, and moves with a slow but powerful force. It is where your conscience lies and your true feelings take form. The heart is resilient and strong, and it is hard to move the heart from what it wants to be. The problem is the heart doesn't read warning signs or imply logic, so without the mind leading the heart, the heart can land in the wrong place and form a bond, clinging to something or someone that is detrimental to its being. Once it is fused there, it is difficult to be moved. For this reason, you must take your time and use your mind to make sensible decisions, before exposing your heart to possible danger and abuse.

Many people live their entire lives using just their minds and hearts, but in order to achieve complete fulfillment in your life, one filled with light from within, you must awaken and involve your spirit. **Your spirit** is where your essence, the very core of you, lives. Your brain is the map, your heart is the engine, but your spirit is your internal compass. It is where God lives within you. Without this compass, no matter how intelligent you are, you can spend a great deal of time going in the wrong direction or making bad choices. The spirit is intuitive – it senses signs, spirits, feelings and omens. It knows which way to go when you have no logic or experience to guide you, and it keeps you safe from the dangers that your eyes cannot see. When you awaken your spirit, everything in your life becomes clearer – good as well as bad. It's like you have been walking around in a fog all this time, and things finally look clear. Your religious or personal beliefs are of no importance here, because the path you take to find your inner spirit is your own. The only important thing is to get there. When you do, you will strengthen your gift of discernment. You'll find your positivity, and strengthen your humanity. The more you utilize your spirit, the stronger your spirit will become and the easier it will feel to hear your inner voice that will guide your life.

When you strive for a balance of these three elements within you, you will begin to feel the warmth of Your Internal Light within your soul. This light is an awakening.

When your mind is illuminated with this light, it is fully aware. It is open and can see things clearly, free from the mental prison of your past, other people's opinions and the past of others before you. It no longer is held back by judgments, confusion, guilt or fear. It is awakened.

When your heart is illuminated, it is full. It is open and warm, and it is filled with love and appreciation for yourself, which in turn allows you to openly love others. It is unburdened by old baggage and misguided attachments. When an illuminated heart loves, it loves without fear. It is free.

When the light of your spirit is awakened, it is the brightest light within you because your spirit is the only part of you that cannot die. Its voice can be heard in your mind, and though it is weightless, it is wise and strong because it is God's light that gives it light, strengthening it with positive discernment and faith. It perseveres when you feel beaten and is undeterred by past failures, pain and disappointment. It is exalted.

When all three elements inside you are in balance and illuminated, your internal elements will actually cultivate and care for each other. The mind and spirit will care for the heart, while the heart and spirit will be selective of what you allow into your mind, as well as your surroundings. It is a circular harmony that nurtures one another. This synergy will become your most valuable asset, and in caring for your elevated consciousness, you will in turn nurture your aspirations, your happiness, your health and your well-being. This internal light is the root of all happiness. It is a conscious state of being, akin to a rebirth. It will enrich your soul and give you a feeling of contentment in your life. And as you live and grow, the light within you will not only grow brighter, but others will also feel it as well, allowing you to spread the warmth of this light to others. The more you feel this internal light, the more you will strive for a higher purpose.

Your present needs or problems may feel so overwhelming that it may seem impossible to find any level of happiness. But you must remember that your entire life is a journey and there are no mistakes – only opportunities to learn, grow, become stronger and move forward. No matter where you are in your life right now, you can achieve peace.

There are things in your life that you already know need to change. You may even know deep inside what you have to do to change them, but you don't know how to begin to do it. How do you leave? How do you stop being afraid? How do you let go? How do you say what needs to be said? How do you take this chance? It all seems so impossible to conquer, but they are not. You just have to go about conquering them differently.

You must first remember that everything you do, choose and feel flows from your internal state. So no matter what problem or external situation exists, the solution must start within you. Even when someone else is at fault. Even when the circumstance is beyond your control. Because once you have achieved mental, internal and spiritual harmony, the manner in which you deal with circumstances or problems will completely evolve. How they affect you will change. How you view it will change. And how much something or someone can dismantle your inner being will completely change.

Once this change takes place, you will have taken control, and the more control you have over your life, the happier you will be. Your aura and energy will brighten, and you will learn that this positive energy not only exists, but is also quite powerful. Through this energy, you will find your will, and you will find your faith. Faith in God's will for you, and faith in yourself. You will no longer fear the unknown, and you will be strong beyond your physical being.

Most importantly, you will know that no matter what comes your way, your life's purpose is within your reach, no matter how long it takes to get there.

And how long it takes is almost always quite sooner than you think.

Lay a Good Foundation.

Every amazing structure begins with a good foundation. Have you laid a good foundation for the life you want? One that is solid and able to withstand being weathered? One that is steady and can allow you to feel peace? People think that if they have done too much in their lives or made too many mistakes, they can't start over. Although we can't change the past, the future has yet to be written. Every day that you wake up is an opportunity to start over. So how do you begin to repair what seems unfixable in your life?

Always Start With You.

When you are feeling unhappy, unsatisfied, or simply want a positive change in your life; no matter what life has dealt you or who seems to be the cause, know that in order to affect positive change, it must always start with you. Many people mistake this approach for assigning blame to yourself. This is not the case. It is simply accepting the laws of life – the only person in this world that you can control is yourself. You can't even control your own children, as they have minds of their own. So waiting for someone else to do something or deciding to stay upset forever because of what someone has done to you, will never affect change. Always look at your options and see what you can do to make a change.

For situations out of your control, you must learn how to change your perspective or find a positive avenue and take that road, not looking back. This of course is easy to say and not so easy to do; all bad situations are not that easy to get over. When devastating things happen in your life, you have the right to, and absolutely should, take the time to feel sorrow – but remember to never stay there. You were not created to live in a state of depression, and you should never give up living because of sadness.

If someone hurt you, they don't deserve that power over you. If you are the one that did the hurting or wronged someone, the only thing you can do at this point is show your remorse, learn from the mistakes you have made, and do better next time. The point is no matter what the situation is, you must keep moving. What you have lost has already happened, and what is meant for you is still waiting. Cherish and value the now. It's all you have, so make the best of it, and get moving. No matter what has happened, more is yet to come, and only you can decide how it will turn out.

Be Aware of Your Intentions.

Life is not simply about your actions, but the intent behind them. Everything you do begins with your intentions. If your intentions are of a good nature, then your path will be protected. It will be guided. It will be led. And it will be encouraged.

When your intentions are not of a positive nature, more of the same will likely come from it. You can't be driven by jealousy and expect real love to appear. You can't be driven by spite and expect to feel accomplished. Negative energy is still strong energy, but in the end you will be void of the happiness you seek, because your intentions were not of the right nature. Your intentions should be pure and filled with good, in order for good to happen to you.

Intentions based on the wrong feelings are not always malicious. One example of this is guilt. You cannot make sound decisions based on guilt; it clouds your judgment and leads you down a misguided path. This often happens with your family and children. Let's say for instance you were an absent or bad parent. Maybe you were a drug abuser. Or maybe you had an abusive spouse, and you feel guilty because you didn't leave soon enough for the sake of your children. If you are now spoiling that child or not giving them the proper guidance and discipline they need because of your past, the only thing you're accomplishing now is making another bad decision that will hurt them in the long run.

As bad as it may make you feel, nothing you do for them now will prevent you from having to swallow your past mistakes. You cannot undo your past mistakes by allowing guilt to make you go against your better judgment. Part of being an adult is owning your mistakes and learning from them. Don't become a prisoner of your past. The past has already been written, but the future still has new possibilities.

Be fully conscious of why you're doing something. Your intentions should be of a positive nature and make sense for you and whoever is involved, so that it can end with a positive outcome.

Feed Your Mind And Spirit.

We know the human mind is where are success begins. Therefore, you must nurture it and take care of its health. We are often too careless with the things we subject our minds to. Reality shows. Fights. Drama. Negativity. Things we call entertainment, that are anything but. Real entertainment is fine, but leave room for the things you need: knowledge, insight, wisdom, courage, and peace. Read books and newspapers. Do puzzles, learn new things. Meditate, laugh, fill your mind with positive people, thoughts and affirmations. Understand that the more you develop your mind and spirit, the more they will work for you. The energy that surrounds you is a very powerful force in your life… including your own. Take care of who and what you allow into your space. Limit or rid yourself of people who submerge you in constant negativity, gossip and drama. This doesn't mean you do not love them. It just means that you have elevated from these things, and choose not to have it in your space anymore. The choices you make in this world can either make your light shine brighter, or dim it. Share what you know, be thankful and help others in need, in order to feed your spirit. The more you share and give, the more good will come back to you.

If you find yourself always expecting the worst, despite many possible outcomes that can be positive and great for you, then it's time to consider a change in your way of thinking. Negative outcomes could be what you are used to, and we are always more comfortable with what we know, even if it's bad. The reason for this is we feel like if we know what to expect, we could protect our hearts better. But this line of thinking doesn't take into account that what you manifest in your mind is also what you put out into the world, and what essentially comes back to you. If you expect to fail, you already have. Living positively and dreaming positively produces positive things. Embrace the thought that you can win and you deserve good in your life, because you do. Good won't just happen, you must go after what you want. So start going after it with your mind: your thoughts, your dreams, your way of thinking. Mentally visualize positivity, so that it can materialize in your life. And always keep in mind that you are worth it.

Get To Work For You.

Unless you are rich or born into wealth, most people have a job. We do these jobs on a daily basis without giving much thought to it; it's simply what we have to do to make a living. Other factors in your life require work as well – your home and your family – yet once again, most of us do these things with no problem, it's simply what must be done. We are good at taking care of everyone and everything: from the house, to the kids, what the spouse needs, making that presentation shine for the boss, walk the dog, clean or take out trash, then wake up and do it all again tomorrow. But when it comes to the future and growth of ourselves – our wants, our dreams, even our well-being – this area, unfortunately, is where most people fail to clock in.

If you are not complete inside, how can you be complete for anyone else? You must consider your happiness as much as everyone else's. And anything worth having in your life requires work. You make time for your job, helping that company to continue to thrive, build and grow. But you should also make time to work on your own body, your mental health, love in your life, your dreams or your own business; things that are more important for you in the long run. Yes, you need money to survive, so you need a job if you don't have your own business or fortune. But when you leave, they will quickly replace you. On the other hand, when your health fails, you only have one body and it cannot be replaced. When you don't put in the work for your wants and dreams, they never happen. And when you don't take time for yourself in general, you live an unsatisfying, unfulfilled life.

The only limits you have in this world are the ones your mind puts on yourself. It's time to start clocking in to the job of YOU, and working towards your own happiness. Your own peace. Your own body. Your own family's quality time. Your own success. Your own dreams. You CAN do both. You're not the first, and you surely won't be the last. So start small at first, even with only one hour out of the 24 you're allotted daily just to do something for you, and see what happens. You'd be amazed at what kind of progress you could make in that hour over time. Then as time goes by, you may find yourself wanting to do more, and even more.

Do well at every job you perform. But also do well at the job of YOU. Otherwise what is it all for? Your entire life should never come down to a company's paycheck.

Take Care Of The Vessel.

Taking care of your body is essential – without the external, there is no internal. We only have one body, we cannot receive another. It houses the mind, and the mind is the foundation for anything you want to accomplish. You can have a strong mind, but without a strong body, you will be limiting your ability to expand your mind's will or desires. This will shorten the bridge that links your mind with what reality can be. So be mindful of taking care of your body. It is the most precious thing you have.

35

Control Your Emotions.

Part of being an adult is learning how to control your emotions. People cannot truly live without emotions. They are the conduit of happiness, sadness and everything in between. But emotions must be controlled, as they are powerful as well as impulsive. We can't truly succeed if we don't have control over our feelings. When we make decisions in our daily lives, there must be a balance of both emotions and stable, logical thought processes that marry each other to come to a great conclusion. Always remember that progress or happiness should never be derailed over temporary feelings. If you are feeling conflicted with a decision, don't make a rush one – this is usually your emotions trying to lead you. Put it aside and give yourself time for your emotions to calm down, and your mind to take over and think things through. More likely than not, the right decision will come to you naturally, and it will be a better decision than the one you would have made in the height of your feelings. Always remember that the damage we can do while feeling anger or hurt is like a rock we have thrown – once we throw it, we cannot bring it back.

Work on Your Balance.

Life is not about extremes on either side of the spectrum. We must find our balance. Slow down to savor and enjoy your life, but don't slow down enough where progress is too slow to make waves. Be courageous and fight for what you want, but also know what to let go of for the sake of your peace. Build wealth so that your life is comfortable, but don't chase money to the point of sacrificing your integrity, loved ones or morals. Try your best to find and maintain balance in all aspects of your life, so that something important isn't lost in the pursuit of something else.

Learn Humility.

One of the most difficult hurdles we face that hinders our growth is pride. We should always be aware that we don't have all the answers, and everything we want to do is not what we should be doing. Therefore, in order to truly get somewhere, we must always be in a state of learning. We do not know where these life lessons will come from, so we must be humble, and keep an open mind.

As we grow in this life, remember that every single being in this world deserves respect. We live in a world where status is important, but a true human being of light knows that every soul has its purpose. We all breathe the same, we all feel love as well as pain, and we can all learn something from one other. Open your mind and your heart to the people and things that God places in your path. You will not only live a fuller life in doing so, but you will also find that in loving others, that love also permeates to love for yourself.

As you go on with life, you'll learn that the person who cannot own the fact that they are human and therefore imperfect, will not go very far. We all make mistakes, and should be able to own them freely, and without limits. Saying "sorry" doesn't make you weak. It makes you strong, confident, and secure enough to own who you are. Saying "I don't know" is an opportunity to learn, and now be in the know! Practice humility – in all you know, and all you learn.

Learning is infinite. There is no limit to what you can learn. Teaching can come from anyone, any age, any race, and any experience. Walk into your experiences and interactions with a humble heart, and you will emerge wiser, smarter, and more fulfilled. When you find yourself in the same problems over and over, it's okay to ask yourself what role you played in this dilemma in your life, and what you need to learn from it or change. If you don't, you will be forced to live the same mistakes over and over again. It's much easier to change for the better if you put things in their proper perspective. You're not changing because you hate who you are, you're changing because you are growing. And everyone, at any age, should always be in a state of growing. We are all imperfect creatures, learning as we go and trying every day to get it right. What comes next is entirely up to you.

Begin positive change with laying a good foundation, and decide that your happiness is more important than your limits. You'll be amazed what will come to you once you decide that failure is not an option. The power you have inside of you is beyond your comprehension. Will your desired life to come out. The result will be nothing short of remarkable.

Realize Where your Power Lies.

Uncovering the limitless power you possess within you to create the life you seek, begins with simply discovering key strengths that have been lying dormant inside of you over time. Once you open yourself up to unlocking and mastering them, the possibilities will be endless.

Find The Power Of Your Mind.

Every single thing in this life that you achieve begins with your mind. Every other factor is significant, but it is not the root of your success. An inborn talent, for example, is just that. It doesn't begin your journey to achieving success, and it is not a beeline to your goal. Not by a long shot. In order to see success from any talent, you must cultivate it, reach for greatness, never give up, and have faith. Amazing physical strength is also great, but it is your mind that pushes you past your normal physical limits to become that strong in the first place. Your mind keeps you trying again after the 50th fall. It keeps you taking the next step forward, after your physical body or even logic has told you to quit. It keeps you up to practice until you get it right, no matter how long it takes. In short, your mind pushes you past what your physical being says is enough. Your physical being therefore has no choice but to become stronger, faster, smarter, better – in order to achieve the new heights your mind has demanded that it reach. This is how you become strong, skillful, and knowledgeable. This is how you achieve and become better than you once was.

So in order to begin this journey, you must begin with your mind. Not knowing where to start is perfectly fine, because simply deciding to change is the beginning of change itself. The rest will come in its due time.

Find Your Driving Force.

Successful people are not geniuses. They simply do what most will not. One of these things as we discussed, is pushing past your normal limits. But there is another factor that you must be prepared for, and that is sacrifice. We must be willing to do the things that are difficult, as well as the things that are uncomfortable. When the things you must do to survive prevent you from doing the things you need to do to win at life, something must change. From a stressful job with long hours to family responsibilities at home, people who have a demanding life must understand that finding the time and strength to succeed is paramount, even if that time and strength sacrifices sleep, rest or relaxation. People who succeed walk the road most don't travel, with the idea that they can relax while feeling accomplished later. But what pulls you out of bed before everyone else? What makes you go to practice instead of staying at home? What makes you keep going even though the road seems endless? The answer is your driving force.

In everyday life, people are usually moved to action by external influences. An example of this is someone who prepares a special meal they would never normally cook on a weekday for guests, or when someone thoroughly cleans up their home because people are coming over. The desire for people to see their house clean overpowers any laziness they may feel.

External influences can even affect your actions over a short period of time, like someone trying to impress a person they recently met. It isn't that they necessarily want to be fake with this new person, it's more so that they want them to see the "best" him or her there is. This does imply, however, that somewhere inside, they know that they don't normally live their best life, and the idea of revealing this to someone new doesn't sit well with them.

External influences generally don't last long enough to fix a problem permanently, unless the external influence has actually moved you internally. Take the person who has never been able to lose weight or keep it off, suddenly now is able to lose that weight because a doctor has informed them that if they don't, they will die. As cold as it may sound, the only element that really changed was their frame of mind — failing was no longer an option. This means they've always had it in them to achieve losing weight, they just needed the proper motivation.

Finding your driving force is the act of finding the motivation to be the best you, without any external influences. YOU are the constant influence. Ever started a great project that you never finished? Started to lose weight, then stopped? Started working on that great new business idea, then it just faded away? Have you ever started great habits for yourself and your health, then slowly fell back into your old routine? Have you ever started to work towards what you've always dreamed of doing, then decided it was just too hard to fit into the life you already have?

Knowing or awareness clearly isn't enough, because deep inside we know what's good for us. We must constantly feel why we're working so hard. What we're so tired of. What we want so badly that the mere thought of it is enough to invoke strong emotions; and the idea of not getting it is enough to wake you up in the morning. Always keep these thoughts in the forefront of your mind. This is drawing strength from your driving force. If you don't do this, after time, when that initial emotion that pulled you in fades, you will become occupied with everyday life, and you will never finish. The key is to renew that driving force to keep you going, so the emotion behind what you are doing is always present, and you can draw strength from it always.

Even with a driving force, just thinking about how hard something is to achieve can discourage you. But understand this: when you are not happy, when you feel frustrated and depressed because you are not where you should be in life or at that moment – the reality is no matter what you decide to do, even nothing, it is ALL hard. If you are in a bad relationship that you know you should walk away from: staying is hard, pleading on deaf ears is hard, arguing is hard, AND leaving is hard. If there is something you're not saying to someone that you know should be said, being quiet is hard, AND saying what needs to be said is hard. If you are avoiding something or someone you should face, running from the situation is hard AND facing it is hard. The reason is no matter how hard you try, you cannot run from yourself. So if you think doing nothing is easier than doing what you know you should, just think about how you feel when you do nothing. Does the problem magically go away? When you are not in balance, every avenue you take will be hard. The difference is one avenue can bring forth change and even happiness down the line, while the other avenue just continues frustration and misery. Why not take the difficult journey that will affect positive change in the end? Life is too short to be unhappy. Even if you're unhappy in silence.

Find Your Passion.

Your mind leads you on a course and your driving force keeps you motivated, but your passion is a source of power that goes beyond these elements. It comes from your innermost thoughts, wants and dreams. Your passion is what makes you tick. It's what makes you come alive when you're doing it, or thinking of it, or even dreaming of it. And when you are, everyone can see that it is what you're meant to be doing. In short, it is your strongest motivation.

The truth is, many people go through life just existing. This simply means that they are not in as much control of their lives as they should be. If you're one of these people, you are mostly taking whatever life brings you, and life isn't always fair. It's actually rather mediocre. Bland. Ordinary. Now, the people who succeed in achieving the things they want outside of the realm of ordinary and inside the world of amazing? They all have one thing in common – they dared to reach for it.

This means reaching for something that is not yet a reality, therefore you cannot yet see, feel or touch it. It only exists in your mind. This person has reached into their soul and found the strength to go after more than what the world thinks is possible, because they can feel just how real it is.

You don't simply work for it – there are hard workers everywhere. You must actually speak your heart and mind's vision into existence, regardless of the things that come to derail you: doubters, failures, roadblocks, fear, etc. Because if you can't see it or think it's possible, then no one else ever will.

If you don't feel like reaching for your dreams is your ONLY option no matter what comes your way, then you might as well quit now. Because as sure as the sun rises, adversity is going to come your way when you go after something you want. This is not a cement wall that you cannot break through, it is simply an obstacle that is meant to appear that way. It is designed to test your limits and determine where your mind is, where your spirit is, and how bad you want what it is you are reaching for. But no matter what comes your way and how impossible it may seem to overcome or get past, if you continue to dare to reach for the dream you have, the vision you see, the happiness you seek; once you harness your energy to reach for it and speak life into it, then all those roadblocks the universe has thrown at you will eventually have no choice but to move out of your way. There is NO question this will happen. The only question is if you are strong enough to keep the dream alive until it does.

Dare to want something more out of your life. You'd be so surprised where that takes you. Or what that one dream can grow into, as dreams do mature and change over time. The mere gravitational pull from your energy makes things happen.

The saying goes "luck favors the prepared." No truer words have been spoken. It doesn't just happen. You have to be focused on it. Aim for it. Desire it. Plan for it. Speak life into it. And reach for it.

Find Your Purpose.

People spend an inordinate amount of time chasing things that they shouldn't. And when you don't realize what is truly valuable in your life, you end up in a constant state of chasing the wrong things and never feeling happy. This is why it is important to find your purpose. When you find your purpose, you also find perspective. Of course we all want to have enough money to be financially secure and comfortable. But this life is about so much more than money. Redirect your energy and chase your purpose. Chase your dreams. Realize your gifts. Chase your passion. When you do, the money will come. Your intentions behind your goal are everything. If you have the right intentions, everything you want will come. If you don't find perspective or get the true meaning of what you should be working hard for, then you will be chasing the wrong things forever, and losing your soul in the process. Examine your intentions and determine if they are the right ones. Then you'll discover your true purpose, and what you should be putting your energy towards. We'll speak more about your purpose later.

Find Your Gift.

We spoke about passion and purpose, let's speak about what ignites these strengths. There are many things we can be good at – even great at – but usually in life, there is one gift we are born with that when we pursue it and cultivate it, the result is phenomenal. This isn't a talent we liked and learned to pick up on – you can have many of those. This gift is one that you've always had within you. It's innate. Some of us are born to be athletes. Some are born to be speakers. Others are meant to teach or write, others still are meant to be builders. The reason why some people never find the type of success or satisfaction they are looking for is because they are going after something that they weren't born to do.

This can be very difficult for many to accept, because everything you want to do isn't want you're supposed to be doing. Often we go after these things because our eyes are looking to something else: the money that comes with it, fame, admiration, etc. You may see someone in a very successful career and say to yourself, "I know can do that," and the truth is, you probably can. You may even be able to make a good living from it. But if it is not your purpose, the type of amazing success or recognition you may be looking to achieve from it will not happen. Because your amazing lies in something else.

And the thing is, that's OK. We are not all meant to be doing the same thing. In a musical performance, everyone is not meant to be the singer; some of us are meant to manage behind the scenes and produce. Others are meant to make the stage lighting look phenomenal, or design the clothes, or manage the sound. There are many pieces of a puzzle that make something amazing, and without even one of those pieces, it would not come together. Whatever your gift is, if you hone in on it and do your personal best, you're not just going to be good at it, you're going to be amazing.

And if you are great at it, people will notice, and you will be more successful at that than anything else you have done or would ever tried to do. Please know that even if that gift isn't one that has you in the spotlight, that doesn't mean you're settling for less. It's you embracing who you truly are, and being the best at it.

Everyone is born with gifts, but the truth is most people don't pursue them. Sometimes it's because the gift is not the most common or sought after talent, or because it's something they don't think people will believe in or think is profitable. But anything that is truly your purpose is something that people can see greatness in. Embrace your calling. Then cultivate it, groom it and develop it. Become GREAT at it. Whatever success you are seeking, you will surely find it in this. You just have to be willing to give it a chance.

When you think of the essence of you – what makes you, YOU – what do you see? I'm not talking about what you like, or admire. You can have a million likes and be good at them. I'm speaking of what makes your heart smile. Something that if money was not a factor or even in the equation, you could still do it forever. It truly does not matter if others can't see your light or vision. It only matters if you can. Because if you can see it, when it blossoms, others will see it as plain as day, and it will be nothing short of amazing. There are countless people in the world leading remarkable lives off of talents and ideas that people never could have imagined would be, until it actually was so.

You may not know how you'll get there. And finding your true purpose in life doesn't mean it will be easy. Nothing worth having or doing usually is. But once you make up your mind that this is where you want to go, where you are meant to be, keep going. Once you do, you will be so surprised at what comes. Your present situation, age, job or career is of no consequence. Happiness knows no age. It only knows the feeling of achievement, and the smile in your heart that comes when you can see the horizon. Your gift is already inside of you. Reach in and begin to cultivate it, strengthen it and make it grow. It will never disappoint you, because if nothing else, it will bring more happiness to your state of mind, and bring more balance to the life you presently lead. And who wouldn't want that.

Find Your Patience.

Finally, you must learn patience. If you believe in your journey, you must also believe in its timing. Accept your path, the stage you're in and the place you are at. You are there for a reason. If you are actively working towards success, not being where you think you should is not an indication of failure; it is simply a part of the road you did not expect. If something you wanted did not come to you, it just means something else is coming. You can't see something better in front of you if you are stuck looking back on what you didn't receive.

Don't think too far ahead with your goals. It will overwhelm you and cause you to stop moving forward, because your mind doesn't have all the answers and therefore cannot reason how you will get there. That's okay. The key is the journey. Always look and appreciate where you are right now, with the future close in your mind. Don't jump ahead. Because you will miss what's in front of you right now. And that's all we have at the moment – now.

When you push through your anxiety and are able to conquer your worry of the unknown, you are truly halfway to your goal before you even start anything physical, because once the mind and will are strong, you already know you will get there. Knowing in your heart and mind that you will succeed is more powerful than anything else. It doesn't matter how long it takes. What matters is you are on your way.

Tapping into these strengths that you possess inside of you and mastering them will make you feel like you have already won, long before you've even reached whatever goal you are going after. And this is indeed the real goal – less confusion, less fear, less bondage; and more control, more courage, more freedom... more happiness.

Refocus your Lens.

The further you reach into yourself, the more you discover layers that have been building up around you and blocking amazing things from coming in. It is then you can experience catharsis and discover healing. But out of all things you may want to improve upon, it is most important to have the proper perspective in your life. If you don't, no matter how much you attain or how good your life is, you will never be happy. Two people can have the exact same situations, yet one can be happy, while the other one is miserable.

The only difference between the two is the way they see the situation in their minds. Your perspective on the things that happen in your life is paramount to your peace. The only thing in this world that you can control is you, so how you react to situations – your point of view, your temper, your patience and your overall disposition – all play a seri-

51

ous role in your everyday life. Although it may feel like it at times, the world is not out to get you. The world really has no feeling about you one way or the other. It is emotionless. That is why good or bad can happen to anyone. This we cannot control. But the energy you put forth, as well as the energy you allow around you, is what enters and lives in your space. And this is something you have a great deal of control over.

Real happiness is simply about changing your perspective. How you view things. How grateful you are for what you already have. How possible you think it is for you to succeed in life. How much you trust and believe in yourself and your journey, even when unexpected things happen. In short, changing your view on life will change everything in it.

The goal is to live a life that doesn't weigh you down. One with dreams and journeys, learning and teaching, as well as love and awakenings. Living a life with the light that lives within you shining brightly. A life that feels complete, even without all the money, or (insert your want here) in the world. Realize, recognize and appreciate what you already have, and put your life into proper focus.

One of our biggest problems as humans is our disrespect for this thing we call time. When things don't happen in the time that we expect it to, we become unhappy. Oftentimes the answer was simply that we should examine ourselves and either do more, fix something, or continue doing what we were already doing and be patient. Most times, we don't examine all the factors.

All we can see is that we really want this thing, and we haven't gotten it yet. That's when feeling sorry for yourself kicks in and things go terribly wrong because we give up, never knowing how close we were to that achievement.

No matter how things appear to be in your life, know that no one in this life is meant to be unhappy, including you. If you've put in the work and feel you deserve to achieve something, keep going after it. You will eventually find the missing link or learn what it still needs in order to get there.

If something evades you that is beyond your control, like finding love or getting married, having a baby, etc., understand that things happen in their own time, not yours. There is nothing we can do about this. Respect time. It exists for a reason and if you don't have something yet, it may be because of a reason that you're unable to see right now, but that will come into focus later.

Know when you're in this situation that whatever is meant for you is already yours. No one can take it from you… except you. If it is not here yet, then use this time to actually be ready for when it does. Because if you rush things that you aren't yet ready to handle, you may end up having a less-than-favorable outcome.

Many of us want to be in a relationship so badly, that we are miserable inside. But can you imagine if the right person came along before you were ready to receive him or her? Before you had gotten over your past relationship? Before you'd matured? If you force things to happen out of their intended time, then you could very well destroy the one thing you've been waiting all this time for, or end up in a situation that wasn't what you wanted at all. If it hasn't come yet, it's not because you don't deserve happiness; it could simply be that there's something you still need to work on inside of you before you can receive it.

People sometimes feel like everything in their life is going wrong. Like nothing, not even one thing (at least that's how it feels) can go right for them. But what they don't realize is everything in your life borrows energy from one another, so therefore everything, big and small, is relative. Everything you do or don't do in this life is a piece of a whole that is the makings of you. One element is not separate from the other – every link in your life connects to the next. So when you think about changing your life, don't get overwhelmed by the idea of huge changes. Start with the little things. These small changes come full circle throughout your life and set the groundwork for bigger, more beautiful things to come.

Begin with the way you think. The way you talk to people. The respect you display to others. Start with your home – it should be in order, the way you want your life to be. Start with your attitude, being grateful instead of cynical. Start with your manner of dress; you want people to take you seriously, so you need to take yourself seriously. Finally, express the love and kindness you want to receive in return. Kindness is free. Words of encouragement are free. A smile is free, but worth so much more to the people you spread it to.

Your attitude is relative to everything. It should be a positive energy that is universal throughout your life. Every person alive has something to be grateful for, and things do not have to be perfect in order for you to have a good attitude. If something exists in your life that is making you act or feel negative all the time, rid yourself of it quickly. Life is too short to spend most of your life being unhappy, and spreading that negative energy to others. If people see you being angry, rude or unfair to someone, people will assess that you are an unkind person, not just unkind in this one situation. Be mindful of your words and actions, and don't be so quick to anger. When you exude humility, respect and fairness, you will get it back positively in multitudes. Your attitude to any situation sets the tone to what you will receive in return. Respect the importance of the right attitude and things will begin to turn around for you before anything else in your life changes.

Your outlook is relative to the people, opportunities and even partner that you'll attract in your life. What your mind already thinks it is, is likely what it will be. Positivity produces more positivity, and negativity does the same. Your negative energy can infect other areas of your life and literally derail your path: derail the right man or woman from coming into your life, derail that job you were meant to get, derail that friendship that should have stayed strong. People who are angry at the world when things don't go their way either don't trust their own journey, or don't have the strength or humility to take a look at themselves and discover what they could do to remedy their situation. What could you have done better in your relationship? When they chose someone else for that job or role, what did they see in them that they didn't see in you? If their choice was based on unfair standards, then they did you a favor; you shouldn't be in that situation anyway. When we search for answers, they come. Wallowing in self-pity, or even resorting to jealousy or hatred will not get you any closer to your desires than where you were before. They are useless emotions. Take control of the things you can, and find patience and trust in your journey for the things you cannot.

When we are caught up in being negative, we can't even see good things happening to us. It affects our entire outlook on things. Changing your perspective will change the way you think about everything – things that aren't that serious, you don't dwell on anymore. Things that are, you take ample time to find out what you could do better next time, or what good can come out of it. And things that are out of your control, you realize are a waste of energy because you cannot control them anyway. Changing your perspective can literally change your life.

When you feel that negative energy taking over—frustration, anger, jealousy, impatience—and you don't know what to do, remind yourself that none of these emotions help you get any closer to what you want. Remember to be grateful. Be thankful for all you have, and how far you have come. Stop to see the distance from where you were before, and where you are now.

If you can't see what you have now and how grateful you should be, chances are you won't be able to fully appreciate the things you get in the future, either. Then you're left in a world where you'll never be happy. And that's a world that no one wants to live in. Change your perspective, and you will forever change your life.

Daily Affirmations and Self-Reflection.

Transitioning your thoughts to results begins with focus. You now know that every single thing you accomplish starts with your mind, so how do we maintain the focus in our minds to get to our goals? The answer is consistency. Consistency builds momentum, and once that momentum is build up over time and becomes a powerful force, nothing can stop you from moving forward. Reward is not something that is quickly gained. It comes from continual, steady effort, and obtaining success and happiness is directly connected to creating better living habits in your daily life.

One of these amazing habits is starting your days with the positive energy that comes from self-reflection and affirmations. This is one of the most powerful habits that immediately begin to improve your state of being. It starts your day with a peaceful and thankful spirit, it prepares you to make accomplishments each and every day, and it keeps your focus alive and bound to progress, which prepares you for the world ahead and the things that try to derail or defeat you every day.

Each day of your life should be filled with accomplishments. And all the little things that you do every day that affect you positively, are accomplishments. It may be something like organizing your closet, or making a call about that debt you've been avoiding, or it could be something like finally starting that savings plan, or starting an exercise regimen. Whatever it is, you should feel like you've accomplished what you've set out to do for that day, even if what you set out to do was to finally get some rest. Start your day by making a mental list of the things you want to accomplish. When you feel accomplished, that energy builds, and you'll find that you'll become more and more accomplished with each passing day.

And an accomplished person is a happier one.

Slowly but surely, these daily goals will begin to grow and become more organized in your mind. You'll begin to see that continuous effort goes a long way, and you'll realize how you can implement that same concept into your life's goals. It won't happen in a day, but it will with consistency. This is where your daily renewals come in.

"But why do I need this magical time to be alone and do this?" you may ask. *"Can't I just make a list?"*

Here's the thing with progress. Real change only happens when you get uncomfortable. When you start making positive changes in your life, your normal habits become disrupted, and it causes your subconscious to rebel against this altering of your already set, continuous pattern. It is not an easy task to create new and lasting habits, and the biggest problem with change is people tend to underestimate the difficulty of this process. It is much easier than you think to slip back into your old ways and put your goals aside, no matter how good for you the change or the goal is. If it was that easy to simply decide to change and it be so, you would have done it already. You must continually keep your mind and spirit strong and focused on what you are doing with daily renewals, affirmations, and goals.

Also, everyday stresses and problems pull us away from peace all the time. In order for you to find your peace again or simply just live a life free from too much stress, you must first learn to quiet the noise in your own mind. Noise does not just refer to sound, it also refers to internal noise: Stress, Worry, Fears, Anger, Resentment, Drama, and Confusion. Quieting all the chaos in your mind is a must before you can change your perspective and move forward in a positive way. Everyone needs time daily to find his or her center. To listen to your inner mind, because it never lies. To quiet the commotion around you and hear your own true voice. It is fundamental that we take time daily to cultivate our thoughts and ideas, suppress our fears, gain perspective, evaluate our actions, be thankful for all we presently have, and find out what we need to do to continually become better. Doing this makes your decisions, choices and direction clearer; it allows you to discern what is important in your life and what's not worth your energy; and it allows you to begin each day with a clear, intentional purpose and resolve. Basically, it's a time to hear all the important things that life's noises drown out. Not only does it affirm what you need to do to improve your quality of life, it also arms you for the unexpected. There is so much in this world we cannot control. We need to be able to control our mind as well as our emotions when the unexpected comes. We begin this by transferring the power of our will and energy to affect positive changes. Once we conquer our worries in our minds, then winning is only a matter of time. All it takes is to begin.

Some people may think of this time as too much to add to their already busy lives. But the difference between going through life and actually taking charge of it, is purpose. The only way you can find and renew your purpose is if you take the time to quiet the chaos around you, so you can discover what you need, then identify and break down the barriers preventing you from getting there. You must take control of your confusion, worries and fears, and find self-awareness, responsibility and acceptance. In turn, you will find your purpose, consistently renew your drive, and find your peace. It is one of the simplest ways you can change the quality of your life.

So where do you begin? Well, it honestly all depends on you. People find their peace in different ways. Some people meditate. Some people pray. Some people take walks or even run in the early mornings or late evenings, where it's just them and the road in front of them. Some people write in their journal. Other people read inspirational books or teachings. Others chant. Some write notes and post them where they can see them, to be inspired and reminded of their words every day. There is truly no one sound process, and it may take you a short while to find out what works for you – but honestly, if you're searching for peace, it won't take you very long. Follow whatever method your heart is drawn to first. When you find what works for you, move forward with it. The result of sticking with this daily routine is maintaining focus, and awakening your inner spirit.

If you still don't know where to start, that's fine. This is all new for your mind. Start with this: First find solitude. The beginning stages of reaching into your mind and soul can involve a great deal of purging, and releasing of frustrations, fear, pain and even guilt. Once that time passes, finding what's comfortable for you will become much easier. Find a place in your home where you are confident no one will disturb you. Outside influences are not conducive, even if it's people you love. This time is only for you. Ideally, it should be done either first thing in the morning to start your day, or it can be the last thing you do at night so you can awaken with it fresh in your mind; but whatever time you can find to yourself will be valuable. Get a pen and a piece of paper – you may want to invest in a journal or notebook. Close your eyes and sit in a quiet space. Your body and posture should feel comfortable, and you should be breathing deeply. Concentrate on your breathing – it's what gives you life and feeds your mind and body. Hear yourself breathing and slowly tune out everything else. Don't think about problems or issues right now. Just try to rid your mind of everything. Do this for a minute or two until a calm comes over you. Now start with first being grateful for all that you already have. It is important to start with being grateful, because gratefulness reminds us that whatever we are going through, there are always things in our present life that are good. So we must be grateful for the things we already have: breath in our bodies, the health we possess, the children we raise or have raised, the love and people in our lives, or whatever else is in your heart that you know you should be grateful for. Start with trying to find a minimum of five things. After you have done this, you are now in the right frame of mind to affirm your purpose.

Affirming your purpose keeps your spirit motivated. Remind yourself that you can do what it is you dream. Remind yourself that it is your calling. It is what you are born to do. It is your future, because it is meant to be so. When you reach the point where your heart is smiling with this reminder, you can then take a few minutes to write down the things you want to accomplish in that day.

Small or big, remember, every accomplishment is a victory, and it will keep your spirit in a positive space. Just think of anytime you've accomplished something you've been putting off for months; no matter how small it was, it's still made you feel accomplished, and amazing. Imagine feeling that every day, or more days than not. Also remember in your daily plans to always be working on something towards your goals, no matter how small. It's okay to even reaffirm that what you have been doing is working and you need to keep going. Writing them down or saying them to yourself helps to organize your day, provide you with focus and lend positive energy to the things you want to accomplish.

Every day of your life should be intentional. It should be a day where you know what you are going to work on or achieve, because if your mind is set on it, it will be that much more attainable. Even days of rest should be intentional. If you start your day with this mindset, it will help you to stay on track, because what you want and need is always fresh in your mind. Start your day with purpose, and lead your day with that purpose in mind.

Often when our lives are full of stress and unhappiness, we can't concentrate on purpose. All we can do is try to get through each day. If this is where you are in your life, then please use this time of reflection every day to first find direction and some semblance of peace. The reason is when you are in a state of turmoil; the wrong energy is present to affect positive change.

You first need to find clarity before finding purpose. The easiest way to do this is to simply start writing what comes to your mind naturally. Sometimes simply being able to let out what is frustrating you is enough to move on. Write it out if you have to. Releasing frustration by writing is very effective. It gives you the opportunity to let it out, then you can leave it right there on the paper and walk away. But if you're too stressed to feel what comes naturally, or whenever the problems in front of you feel too confusing or too much to fix, remember to start with gratefulness, even in times of stress – actually, especially in time of stress – then take a long breath, and ask yourself some simpler questions. Start with basic questions and find those answers, then move on to bigger questions until you find all the answers you need. *What is stopping me from having peace right now, or from feeling fulfilled? What is hurting or frustrating me?* Be as descriptive as you can. After you've done this, you must now own your part in this problem. Yes, yours. The only person you can control in this life is yourself, so the only person you can control to affect change in your life is you. Find out what you can do, not anyone else. So the next question is: What has been your role in this present situation? What could you have done better? Finally find solutions: What can you do to fix this?

If your problem or stress is caused by something you don't have any control over and cannot change, then you must let it go. Stressing over things we cannot change is a wasted emotion, and robs us of other forms of happiness in our lives. This doesn't mean giving up, it simply means that if we are not in control of it, we must learn to let go and move on with life, despite what it is. If it is pain that you must go through, then allow yourself to do this so that you can one day be stronger. Once again writing your thoughts down and purging helps with this. If the problem is that you don't know what to do in a situation, don't give up. Know that any issue you've been feeling confused about, you already have the answers you need – they just haven't surfaced yet, and maybe that's because you've haven't yet learned how to search for them in the right way. But they are within the inner makings of you. You simply have to reach into yourself to find them.

When you're confused about something, remember to go back a little further, or ask yourself simpler questions. Even in heavy situations, simpler questions lead to better dialog, and opens up your mind to thoughts you didn't at first realize. You simply need to get the momentum going. Take your time and as many days as you need to get to the heart of your stress, then decide what you need to do to fix it, so you can move on to bigger and better things. If it takes some time, that's okay, too. When you aren't getting the answers you're looking for, the best thing to do is to leave it alone for a while, and revisit it later. While you're looking for an answer, wait to act. It's better to wait for an answer than to do something impulsive. Just know that when the answers start coming, you need to be willing to listen to them.

Once you have cleared your mind and opened up your heart to receive what answers you need, believe that it will come. And remember that simply choosing to live the life you want is the beginning of happiness within itself. Once you feel that you have found a less stressful place within you, then you can begin to walk into your purpose. And in this purpose, your light begins to shine.

Ask yourself some simple questions: If I could narrow down three things in my life I have control over that would improve my well-being and state of happiness, what would they be? Then for each of these things, ask yourself: How much better would my life be if I accomplished this, and why? What is in my way or stopping me? What am I afraid of? How much am I willing to do to get or achieve this? Dwell on those answers. Your mind will be opened to the possibilities of something new, if you let it. And more questions and affirmations will come as you keep going. All you need to do is to allow the energy to grow. Once the momentum starts, the right questions you need to answer will also come, and your journey to a better state of mind will begin. You don't have to have all of the answers right away; you just have to be brave enough to say, *"I'm ready for change in my life."* The rest will come. Even if you're not 100% sure, that's okay. You may change direction as answers come to you along the way; that's okay, too. It's all part of your own journey. And it's all what you were meant to do. Maybe you had something to gain in the first direction before changing course – like someone to meet, or knowledge to attain.

An accomplished day where you've achieved everything you set out to is a great one. A day where you feel thankful for the things you have is a great one. A day where you feel free of a problem you held on to for a long time is a great one. Only positive things can come from your daily affirmations and self-reflection. Above all things, it is a powerful thing to feel peace, gratefulness and accomplishment every day of your life. If you do, you are already winning.

Trust and Forgiveness: It Is Possible.

As you work towards a better you, a big part of repairing yourself internally is being able to forgive the people who have wronged you, and learning how to trust again. Holding on to hatred for someone who hurt you slowly eats away at your soul, and does a world more damage to you than the person who wronged you in the first place. But even for those who can forgive, trust feels like such a faraway emotion for so many adults. For countless individuals, it feels impossible to trust again after trust has been broken. But trusting again is something you definitely can accomplish.

Why is it so hard to trust again? Well, betrayal is one of the most hurtful experiences you can suffer through when you have loved someone. It can happen to you with all types of loved ones – significant others, friends, relatives, even your children. Once someone experiences the core pain from a betrayal – especially from the person you're supposed to be spending the rest of your life with – it will not only affect that relationship, but can also change your entire outlook on potential loved ones in the future, or even other people in your life. For some, they never want to trust anyone, or even love someone that much again.

For others, they may actually want to trust again, but have no idea how to do it. How do you trust and believe that someone will never hurt you, when you know first-hand how possible, and devastating, it actually is? If the person that hurt you is the one you're trying to trust again, it makes the task in front of you even harder. Not only is it possible that they can hurt you, but since they've done it before, in your eyes it's even more likely that they'll do it again. Trusting is no doubt a difficult job, but it is possible. Though in order to do so, you'll need to actually change your outlook on the word trust. We will focus on the trust of a spouse/partner, but much of this can be applied to other relationships in your life as well.

If the person you're presently with has never betrayed you or given you reason, yet you still constantly experience feelings of mistrust, trust is the way that your fear has manifested itself in your relationships. Though the most thought of, it's not just the fear of cheating, or feeling this person will do what the last person did. You may find that fear has crept into your mind in many different ways: Fear that this person won't love you the way you love them; Fear that they are only with you because of some ulterior motive; Fear that this person will somehow take advantage of you; or Fear that this is temporary and will not last.

Fear and mistrust can present itself even when the relationship is going really well. After the pain you've experienced in the past, the idea of a good, true relationship can feel foreign to you, so when you're actually in one, fear births feelings of 'this is too good to be true,' or 'if it is true, it surely won't last.' Depending on your imagination and level of fear, there can be an unlimited amount of situations that you can conjure up to justify your lack of trust in your relationship, even when no real reason exists to feel this way. But no matter how unsubstantiated, the fear you feel is real, and you feel and think it all the time, so how can you overcome it?

Let us first understand that trust is not an option in a successful relationship. If you don't have trust, then your relationship is just a hollow shell waiting for an imminent breeze. You must trust if you want your relationship to work, and you must have trust in order to form a bond strong enough to withstand the chaos of the world that you live in. If you truly love this person, you want it to work and they are actually worthy of your love and trust, then you must find a way to extend your trust to them.

Let's start with redefining our idea of trust.

What do people want from you when they ask for, or even expect, you to trust them? Do they want you to believe that it is impossible for them to hurt you? Or maybe they want you to believe that everyone else is capable of hurting you, but because he/she loves you, they never will? If we think about it, that is hardly logical, and when we set unrealistic expectations, hurt is almost inevitable. The truth is, we all do and have done things that could potentially hurt someone else. We all have done things that we may not be proud of, and many of us have truly made mistakes we wish we could take back.

So believing someone is incapable of hurting you is not a realistic perception of trust. Therefore, the first step is to understand that trust is not a guarantee that someone won't or can't do something wrong that will hurt you. Trust is not an absolute power. It is not an assurance that nothing can go wrong, even in a great, strong relationship. Nothing is. It can't be, simply because we are not perfect creatures. But that should not stop you from granting someone the same gift of trust that you'd want them to grant you.

Let's dwell on that word, "gift." Trust is indeed a gift – both for the person you are giving it to, and for yourself. Yes, yourself! When you don't have the ability to trust, does it not affect your life greatly? Do you not feel hindered and alone? When you can trust, you feel free, like the weight of constant doubt and insecurity, as well as the inability to truly love is gone.

When you value trust as a gift, you also realize that such a gift is something that you must be choosy of who you give it to, because when you give your trust to someone unworthy of it and it gets broken, you know how difficult it is for you to gain that level of trust for anyone again.

When you trust, you are essentially giving someone a part of you that says to them, "Based on what you have shown me, I am giving you the opportunity to be a part of my life, and do what you think is right by me." It is a privilege you're granting to someone that you believe is worthy of this trust, with the level of trust being based on behavior they have already demonstrated on a consistent enough basis.

Sounds off? Well, let's think of an example. When a parent first puts trust in their teenage child to drive the car, sleep out, or even have an unsupervised party, they are not doing it with the thought that because they love their child, nothing can go wrong. They are doing it based on the behavior that the teen has demonstrated, which allows them to believe that he/she is worthy of this type of trust. A parent loves you, but they often will not let their love for you cloud their judgment when it comes to trust. They will not grant you that level of trust until you have shown consistent signs that you have the ability to be responsible, or are mature enough to handle it. Then with time, if the child continues to act responsibly with the trust already given, they are given more privileges, and higher levels of trust.

Similarly, before you jump out there and put all of your trust in someone, this person needs to show you, over a considerable amount of time, that they are worthy of this gift of trust that you are giving to them. This doesn't mean they are perfect. They have faults just like you do. But they should have demonstrated to you over time that they possess integrity, morals, and genuine love for you, and understand what it takes to nurture this relationship.

More often than not, disloyal people that we encounter will actually show us several signs of not being worthy of our trust. They cannot help it — eventually who they are will shine through. But because of our emotions or other wants, many people put their trust in these unworthy people anyway. We must remember that love, lust and attraction are not the same as trust. You can certainly love someone without trust. This happens with family members all the time. You know their life is a mess and they are not reliable or trustworthy, but you love them anyway.

But if you did this in a relationship, should all the blame be on the other person when they eventually do something you knew they were likely to do in the first place? If, let's say, a business owner hired someone to work in his store who was constantly showing signs of dishonesty, would we not feel like the owner should share some of the blame when the employee eventually does something unsavory? We as humans have no problem being careful with our possessions —our car, our home, our money, etc., and find it easy to be selective with who we trust with these things, but in the same breath, we tend to neglect our own being and can be careless with who we let into our lives, as if our hearts or well-being are not the most important things we possess. When we allow feelings like attraction, lust, loneliness, and low self-esteem to cloud who we should give our gift of trust to, we must take responsibility for what the result eventually is.

Now trust has two stages: It begins with you extending trust to someone, then it continues with that level of trust growing naturally over time, based on the person's care of it, and their ability to remain trustworthy. You don't just jump in with both feet. Your gift of trust should grow organically, and with ease.

But how to do we even begin this trust? Let's begin the act of trust with a healthy spirit, heart and mind. The answers of who or when to trust should come from what you feel deep inside of you. Your internal energies should be guiding you, so that you can first trust yourself. They then will give you discernment for who and when you should trust someone else. For all of this to be effective, you should be complete and internally balanced before looking to trust. If your internal energies are in a state of chaos, how can you make a sound decision on trusting someone?

If you are not in a good place internally, looking for a relationship is not only unfair to the both of you, but your reasons for trusting this person will be skewed based on what you are presently struggling with in your own life; whether it be loneliness, low self-esteem, heartbreak, or something else. When you are in a healthy place internally, and have felt and experienced the assurance of trusting yourself, then you will be able to confidently venture out and trust someone else.

Always remember to respect the gift of trust and how it feels to not have the ability to do so. If you do, you will appreciate the fact that you need time to make a sound decision, and not rush the process. There is no handbook for when to trust, but there are always signs that help you know who to trust, if you take the time to look for them. We just have to love ourselves enough to actually listen to when your spirit says to walk away, as well as when it says to stay, step out on faith, and give it a chance.

All of this sounds great, but how can we really tell when it comes to people? What if we are wrong? The hardest trust to attain is for yourself, because if you've been hurt, you realize that clearly, you've been wrong before. But one positive thing about the truth is it's hard to conceal for an extended period of time.

There are always signs of what the truth really is, because that is simply the makings of truth – it is constantly fighting to break free from the pretense and lies. It's like a stench being masked by cologne – although you smell the cologne, the undertones of what is underneath is still seeping through, if only you'd take the time to allow yourself to discover it. As time goes by, the foul smell will eventually find its way through. No matter how much a person tries to hide it, the truth cannot be contained. Often when we are "fooled" by someone who hurt us, we really weren't fooled at all. It's more that we really wanted to be with this person, so we ignored the signs that were in front of us. Once you have the right balance internally and truly love who you are, the truth becomes much harder to ignore.

So often, it's not that the truth doesn't show itself, it's that when it's in front of you, you have a choice. You can either ignore the truth because you don't want to accept it, or you can acknowledge the truth, know you are more than what this situation has become, and make a decision based on all the facts. It's never easy when you really want something, but when you love yourself more than you want this person or situation, you tend to make the right choice.

What if you know this person should be trusted, but you just don't know how to trust anymore because of past betrayal? The answer to learning how to trust, is to simply start doing so. Trusting is an ability. Like any other ability, when you don't use it or choose not to exercise it, the inner makings of it become weak, and your ability to use it deteriorates to the point where it feels like it doesn't exist anymore. You have to use it and practice it to make it stronger. Start off small: work on trusting someone with little things, in small doses. Trust is not the absence of fear, but you must find the courage to push through the fear you're feeling, if you feel this person is worth it. Over time, that person's actions should help that fear to diminish slowly on its own.

Now it's important to say that when it comes to trust, the fear you feel should only be of the unknown. If the person you're with is doing the same bad things over and over, and you feel fear to trust them, this is not an inability to trust. Your spirit is simply warning you of what you already know is the truth. Innate fear is meant to protect you and keep you cautious. If you already know what is coming because this person continually shows this behavior to you, your internal energies are simply trying to protect you from the inevitable. Don't confuse the two and use your poor choice to stay and be hurt repeatedly, as a reason to no longer trust.

When someone has not yet demonstrated trustworthiness to you (like a stranger, or someone you haven't gotten the chance to really know), or maybe you have decided to give someone a chance that you believe has made a mistake, please know that this is not trust. It is important to be fully aware of your actions, so that you can always be at peace with them. This action cannot be "trust" because the reality is you do not trust them. What you are doing is choosing to step out on faith. Under the right circumstances, stepping out on faith can be a wonderful thing, and at some point in our lives, we all need someone to believe in us. But only your spirit can tell you when that right time is. When doing so, let it always be a conscious decision, so that you can be at peace with whatever the result is, even if it's not what you wanted it to be.

If you have made up your mind to forgive someone that has hurt you and you step out on faith, after time, when they have demonstrated their willingness to atone for their mistakes and change, then the biggest thing you must work on is not living in the past. Keeping in mind that you are not perfect yourself, the further this person moves away from that mistake and has truly grown as a person from that experience, you must recognize the time they have earned for your relationship to flourish. Recognize the person they are becoming, and don't continue to look for the person that made that mistake. Trust can be regained, but know that it is a two-person effort. No matter how much someone has grown or learned from their mistakes, if you only choose to concentrate on the bad they've done in the past, your relationship will never move past it. So keep this in mind when deciding to forgive. If you're not going to truly give the person a chance to move past the situation (or you feel you can't), then you need to make the decision to let them go. Holding on because of feelings will only make you both unhappy in the end.

But whose fault is it when you do trust someone and something goes wrong? Often we assign the blame of someone hurting us to ourselves. That responsibility can have merit if we did not choose our partner carefully, or was not ready on the inside to seek a partner. But if you did your due diligence, followed your spirit and did what you should do in a relationship and this person still hurt you, then that blame is theirs to carry, not yours. Their actions should never result in you not trusting again.

If you give someone your trust, remember that you are giving them a gift. It's something you don't have to give them, yet you chose to anyway. If they did not properly care for that gift, then they need to live with whatever they've done, as well as whatever consequences that come with their actions. Yes, it hurt you, but if you are complete, you'll know that hurting you was more their loss than your own. Feel at peace with your decisions, it's the other person that must answer for their wrongdoings. If you have chosen to forgive someone who's hurt you, there's no need to fear what they might do in the future.

If a repeat offense does happen, with the energy that you've chosen to put out into the universe, it will come to light. It always does. And honestly, it really isn't the worst thing for you. They've already hurt you, and you got through that. If they've chosen to squander the one chance that you've given them to atone and do right by you, then you could now feel relief in knowing that you followed your spirit and gave them the chance that you felt your relationship deserved. If you must walk away now, you can do so with no regrets. People are worried about looking or feeling foolish because you gave someone a chance. Why on earth should you feel foolish? That is what you were supposed to do, give your relationship your all. Part of your all is forgiveness.

If you chose to give them another chance and they did not grab that precious opportunity with both hands, who is really the fool? Now they have lost you, whom they can never replace. And they have to live with the consequences of their actions. You will move on, learn from this relationship and be better for the next person, who will have the gift of you that the previous person foolishly gambled with, and lost. To never love again because someone else did you wrong is simply foolish and insane.

Your heart it is one of your most prized possessions. It is one of the things you should invest in daily, to ensure your happiness. If someone comes in and hurts you, shutting it down doesn't make sense for you, because living without love is not a complete life. Trusting is not a weakness. Being too weak to honor someone's trust, to own what you say and commit to someone you claim to love is the true weakness. Let them go, and move on to bigger and better things. Find someone actually worthy of your heart, and your trust. If it takes you a while to trust again, that's okay. If you are more careful this time before going all in, that's okay, too. It takes a better person to walk away from every relationship stronger and wiser, instead of broken and bitter.

Too many people have the same relationship with different people over and over, but never take the time to learn what they should from it, so they could grow, and shine. You should humbly learn from your bad relationships, not wallow in them. Be that better person, for your own happiness.

Still not there yet? Trust still feeling too difficult to do? Then you must be willing to dig a little deeper.

For some, the idea of opening themselves up to be hurt in the same way they were before seems insane, illogical, and simply not an option. But let me share something with you that you may not know. When you first begin to love, often at a young age, it's all so new and innocent that being careful isn't in the forefront of your mind.

More often than not, you first start to love and trust someone with complete abandon. You don't make sound decisions on who to trust, and you don't even think about how or why you should trust someone – you just do, because you love them. So when that person hurts you and your heart breaks, it hurts like no other pain you've ever felt in the world. It shakes you to your core.

After time passes and you somehow get over what you thought you never could, all you can feel is the determination of making sure that no one is ever able to hurt you like that again. We are self-preserving creatures by nature, and if something or someone hurt you significantly, neither your mind nor your heart will want to venture down any road that looks similar to the one you were on when that pain took place. But the beautiful thing about humans is our ability to become stronger as things happen to us. Much like our bodies get stronger when we put it through something difficult, our minds and hearts also repair and strengthen themselves, so the next hit isn't as hard.

The truth is you can get hurt by love again, but no one can ever hurt you the way you were hurt the first time. Your heart and mind are stronger now. You are more resilient, and you also now know what can happen. That is the gift and the curse that heartbreak brings. It hurts us, but it also makes us stronger. So never be afraid to love or trust again, or let go of the baggage you've been holding onto. The past is just that. Don't live in it. It weakens your spirit, as well as your ability to make good decisions. Instead, use your past experiences to make you smarter in your choices and behavior, so that your path can change. Just because it was your past doesn't mean it's your future. As a matter of fact, you should ensure that your past would never be your future, because you now know what to avoid.

So this fear of repeating the worst pain you've ever felt is a fear you don't have carry, because it is not possible. Find comfort in those thoughts. The most powerful thing you can do after heartbreak is find someone deserving of the love you have to give, and who will treat you the way you deserve to be treated.

The Obsession Of Being In The Know.

Often in relationships, people's display of mistrust has nothing to do with the person they're with or anything they've even done to warrant it. It has to do with the fear of them not knowing something. This fear almost always comes from experience. You see, it's one thing to handle an indiscretion, but it's something completely different to accept that so much was going on, and you had no idea. You truly thought everything was okay. It makes you question everything, including yourself. How could you have missed so much? It's a feeling that people (understandably) never want to happen to them again. So because of this, they often try to be in the know by invading their significant other's personal space. This invasion of privacy is unwarranted and puts an unhealthy strain on relationships. But that fear of not knowing overpowers any logical reason, so people spend a great deal of time snooping, questioning, spying and double checking information, reasoning with themselves that if there's nothing to hide, then they're not doing any harm.

The problem with that is your energy is a powerful thing. Therefore, whatever energy you put into your relationship is the energy you will get back. Anything can look like whatever you want it to, if you're looking at it through a certain set of eyes. If you want information you come across to look good, it will, and if you want it to look bad, it will. Often we don't see what we aren't willing to, and other times we see what isn't even really there, because we already believe it, no matter what the person does. So understand that your snooping isn't bringing you any closer to being in the know. It's only feeding your fear and insecurities, and putting negative energy into your relationship.

Anything in this world that you are supposed to know, you do not have to go looking for. The truth will come directly to you. You'd be amazed at how the truth finds you, but it always does. You just have to be willing to see it when it comes, with both eyes open. So let go of the fear and have faith in yourself, your relationship, your decisions, and the power of truth.

Finally, believe it or not, forgiveness is one of the cornerstones of trust. If you still haven't let go of the negative feelings you've had for someone from your past, that pain will still be lingering in your heart and your actions will reflect that pain, making trust feel impossible. Your mind will still be thinking of what could go wrong or what is probably already going wrong that you don't know about yet—that's what happened the first time, right? Staying in this mental space will only keep your spirit in turmoil. You must first forgive the past and rid yourself of the pain that lives in your heart, in order to open yourself up to receive love again.

So let's go into this section with an open mind, and an open spirit.

Forgiveness.

You'll find as you grow in your journey in life that the properties of true positivity are very much connected to each other. You must achieve one to obtain the other, and so on. It is an infinite cycle. So keeping that in mind, we cannot talk about trust without talking in depth about forgiveness.

Just as trust is something hard to attain, forgiving someone who has hurt you is sometimes equally as hard, or even harder. Unfortunately, one element cannot come without the other. Your energy is singular, and connected throughout all of your life. You can't release positive energy in one aspect of your life and negative energy in another. You will be in a state of conflict if you try, and eventually, one form of energy will become the dominant in your life. Achieving forgiveness is far from impossible. Let's first evaluate why people find it so hard to forgive, in order break down these barriers and achieve a more positive existence.

People often associate forgiveness with giving someone a "free pass" – or basically minimalizing the hurt that someone has put you through because of their actions. One of the reasons we do not forgive is because we feel like if we do, we are basically sending a message that what this person has done to us was not a huge deal. And after all the pain that this person has made you feel, it simply feels like too much to ask you to let it go, like it didn't hurt your heart the way it did, or even alter your life the way it did.

After you endure the horrible experience and the pain has subsided (but not disappeared), a combined feeling of anger, resentment and darkness is what comes next, with the core pain of it all rearing its ugly head on occasion. We hold on to this darkness and anger not only towards the person that hurt you, but also towards the situation itself that surrounded this pain. We now never want to trust again, we never want to love again, never want to be that close to a friend again, etc.

Believe it or not, the dark feeling we are left with, even though it hurts, is actually a comfort to many people. Long after the person that hurt you has gone on with their life (after they've shaken yours), it almost feels like this anger, this pain, this decision to NEVER forgive this person, is really the only thing that continues to validate why we were hurt in the first place. Basically, it keeps the actions that they did to us alive. Understand that we don't want to keep it alive because we are mean and hateful. We want to keep it alive because the idea of something being discarded and forgotten about that impacted your life so much, feels like it is also diminishing all of the pain that you endured. Like it didn't matter. Like it was nothing. And after they've hurt you so badly, how can you let something like forgiveness give anyone the idea that everything is okay, when everything is so very far from being okay?

Well I'm here to tell you that forgiveness is not that at all. Forgiveness is not a free pass. It's also not a guarantee that you will continue a relationship with this person, or even talk to this person again. Forgiveness is honestly not even for the person's benefit that hurt you. Forgiveness is simply you personally declaring to yourself that you will no longer harbor ill feelings or stay in a dark place because of the pain that someone has caused you. That is all. You're not saying it was okay. Clearly it wasn't if it hurt you this bad. You are not saying it doesn't still hurt. You are not even saying everything is okay between the two of you. What you are doing is making a conscious decision to let go of the pain it's causing you. The anger. The resentment. The negative feelings that live inside of you every day and affect your choices, your decisions, and your life. That is what you are letting go of.

You're not forgetting the action. You could never forget what someone did to you anyway, and quite frankly, you shouldn't. It's what teaches you and what makes you stronger. But letting go of the pain is releasing it from your spirit, and from your heart.

Forgiveness and staying with someone do not go hand in hand. You do not have to keep someone in your life in order to forgive the wrong they have done to you, and the only person that can determine if you should or even could stay is you. But know that if the offense was too damaging to your relationship to remain together, then losing you is worse than any other action you could do, or words that you could ever say.

Many people wonder how forgiveness could be for their own benefit. But you are the person hurting, angry, and resentful. You are the person afraid to let someone in again, or living with only half of the happiness you deserve. How is holding on to this pain hurting them as much as it's hurting you? It's simply not. You have to forgive and let it go, or it will continue to eat away at your soul, and affect any new relationship you get into.

The rules for forgiveness are not what people think. You don't have to give anyone a call, or make an announcement. Since this is for you, you just have to make the decision inside of you to leave the hurt there and move on. Simple, just not so simple. The hurt and sometimes hate you feel seems to take on a life of its own inside of you. You feel like you're doing something for them that they don't deserve. But it's never for them, always remember that. It is simply you taking back the power they took from you. You can do this not only for relationships, but also for family or friends that hurt you as well, even someone who has committed a crime against you. You may think you never can, but know that forgiveness is freedom. Let it go, so you can receive the gifts that await you.

Some things you may have held onto for a long time — maybe even years. And the dark feelings you have almost feel like a part of you. You may not even know how to let it go after so much time has passed. But really all you have to do is declare it and mean it, for it to be so. Once you do, you'll soon realize that these dark feelings aren't all that you have at all. You have a life to live. A life that can be filled with good people, lots of love, positivity and happiness. They have hurt you, but they have not broken you. Where you go from here is completely up to you.

If saying "I forgive" is still too much for you, then don't. Only you know the pain that someone has put you through, and what your heart is willing to do. But what you can do is say, "I have to let this go. I have to move on because I will not allow this person to take more from me than they already have. And every day that I am suffering is another day that I am not allowing anyone in; that I'm allowing this person to prevent me from truly living — and that's another day that they have taken from me. So I have to leave this here, and walk away, so I can live again, or truly start living for the first time in my life."

We all have had experiences that have caused us pain. But until you face them, you'll never conquer them. You may think if you cover up your pain and put it in the back of your mind, it will go away. But it never will. It will always be just one layer away from your consciousness; still alive, still thriving, and still affecting your decisions, your emotions, and your ability to love again. The only way to take back that control is to face them. You have nothing to lose and every-thing to gain. Once you have faced them, know that this is not the determining factor for your life, unless you choose it to be. Always remember in your worst pain that you are still here, so they haven't broken you, and that is the biggest light in your truth.

But what about when the person you're angry with is yourself? We are oftentimes our worst critic, and our worst judge. There are people who let guilt dictate their lives. But just as we are to forgive others, we must forgive ourselves. Is it easy? Absolutely not. Sometimes you are the hardest person for you to forgive, but you must. Sometimes the ac-tions we did were because we didn't know any better at that time, or even that age. Other times we allowed some-thing (or someone) to get a hold of our lives and have too much control over our decisions.

Whatever the reason, we are no longer the person we used to be. We have grown, and would never make those same mistakes again. The biggest waste of energy is exert-ed in trying to control things that we cannot change. So if you cannot change it, what can you do? You can take back control of your life, face your mistakes, learn from them and grow from them. You are still here for a reason, so be the best person you can be at this point in your life right now. Because now is all you have, and this life is the only one you have to live.

Trust and forgiveness are not easy things to find and hold on to, but nothing worth having ever is. It may take time, but once you conquer this hurdle in your life, your soul will be lighter, freer, and warmer for it.

And you will be closer to happiness.

Become a Conqueror.

The Internal Light

Win Past the Fear.

Fear is an emotion that everyone possesses. Even babies are born with the fear of falling. Your instincts naturally contain a reasonable amount of fear because it is meant to warn you of approaching danger and move you to react, ensuring your safety or survival. This type of fear is healthy for your life.

But your heart and mind should never be consumed or overwhelmed with fear. In this manner, fear can take more control over you than is deemed healthy – and once it does, it can become a powerful, crippling emotion. Fear displays itself in your life through many forms: distrust, confusion, procrastination, self-doubt, and more – but at the root of it all, it is fear that has killed goals, dreams and progress dead in their tracks more than any other obstacle. Often when we are not even willing to take a chance or go after something, it's not for lack of abilities, talent or even our chances at succeeding – it's because of our fears. And somehow, the fear seems to worsen the closer we get to accomplishing something. People have no idea how close they've been to succeeding when fear set in and overwhelmed them into giving up.

Fear breeds worry, anxiety, insecurity, anger, and even jealousy. Yes, jealousy! Do you think if you really believed you would find your own success, it would bother you if someone else succeeded in their dreams? Do you think if you were completely secure in your relationship and what you have built, it would bother you if your mate admired a quality that someone else displayed? Jealousy can actually be a product of your own fears. In many ways, it's your self-doubt manifesting, unsure of your own abilities. Why else would someone else's success or talents feel like it is simultaneously taking something from your own?

What this person is missing from the experience is that positivity is a saturating energy. If you are friends with a successful person, it can only do you good, because if you let it, it will lend the right type of energy – pride, encouragement, even knowledge – to the things that you are trying to achieve. You should actually be proud that this type of person is attracted to you and your qualities. Invite this type of positive, forward-thinking energy into your life, and welcome successful people into your space always.

When fear manifests itself into self-doubt, it can be very dangerous. Lost confidence in who you are or what you're capable of is beating you before failure has even crossed your path. We all have fear when we take risks, and no success is without risk. But when fear overwhelms you before you have even started put forth an effort, you don't even have a chance of getting to your desired goal. So many things trap us in this fear, and most of the time, we try to deal with fear in silence. No one wants to say they're too afraid to try and fail, or to love and get hurt, or even to start a whole new career or pursue a dream. But who isn't afraid when they do these things? If we didn't keep it to ourselves, we'd soon learn that we are not alone, and may even get help in conquering it, because you cannot conquer what you won't face. So how do we get over this overwhelming feeling, to reach our desired path?

Fear is natural, so it's not something you can just do away with. But you must learn to channel your fear so it empowers you, instead of crippling you. Some people don't even realize that fear is controlling their lives, as it can be very subtle. But if you have stayed in the same place mentally, physically, or emotionally for an extended period of time and never feel motivated to go after the things you really want, you may be more consumed with fear than you realize. Your thought process could be that this is a familiar space that feels secure, and if you give it up for the unknown, you could lose everything. So you stay planted in the same place indefinitely.

That's what fear does. It makes you not want to move towards anything new at all, no matter how good the "new" can be for you. But let's follow this logic for a moment in order to conquer it: The fact is, there is risk and chance in every single thing we do in this life, every single day. If we don't take on any risk, we'll never get anywhere. For example, if we harped on the fact that there is a chance we could get hit by a car when we left our homes every morning, we would never go anywhere. But there is in fact truth in that statement – anything could happen when we leave our homes, including a car accident.

Now imagine if you followed through with this logic and always stayed at home to be accident free. You'd be safe from that, but what kind of life would that be? You'd never experience even the basic things the world has to offer – you'd never see the sun rise, never visit friends, never feel the waters of the beach, never experience a new place, restaurant, or city... you'd never see the stars. No one wants to give all this up, so the majority of people deal with this risk, and a million others, in order to live a normal life.

So if we decide to deal with normal risk for everyday life, why not deal with risk for the things you really want as well? If you never allow someone into your heart for fear of being hurt, or if you never go after any of your dreams for fear of failure, sure you'd be "safe" from what could go wrong, but you also will never truly live the life you were meant to live. Fear is an energy that once you give it life, it can continue to grow all on its own. You can very quickly find that fear has paralyzed your forward movement and left you completely stuck in one place. Whether it's a problem you don't want to face, an opportunity that you don't want to pursue, or even love that you won't let happen, fear can paralyze your progress. All because of thoughts that have run away from you, and you can't seem to reign them back in. How can this be good for you? You would have allowed fear to give the "possibility" of something bad happening too much weight over all possibilities. And your life is too valuable for that.

Here is the truth: None of us can predict the future. We don't know how successful we will be, or how well our children will do in life. We don't know if something will work that we've tried, we don't know if anyone will like what we invented, and we don't know if this person will love us back or even be true. But one fact stands true, regardless of all these things: If we never try to do anything or take a chance and reach for anything, we will also never know what it feels like to win. We must push past our fears and allow ourselves to at least have a chance at winning. Because no one ever regretted trying and failing. They only regretted not trying at all. Even though it doesn't feel like it, fear can be controlled. Remember that fear is simply a feeling, a thought in your head. And if you can change your way of thinking, you can control fear so you have time to concentrate on what really matters: today and now.

Some people get so overwhelmed with not knowing how they are going to achieve their goals that they frustrate themselves out of even having any. But part of the process of achieving a goal is being brave enough to make a goal in the first place. You may not know how you are going to achieve it, but that's okay. Making the goal helps to strengthen your resolve, and the universe will listen. If you don't know where to start, then just start wherever you think you should, and think about it one step, one decision, one day at a time. Once you take the first step, then evaluate where you are right now, and think of the next step. Don't think too far ahead, it will overwhelm you. Let the story slowly form itself, one day at a time. This goes for anything you feel fear with. Beginning the action of going after what you want actually pulls energy towards it; so starting off in the wrong direction really doesn't matter. As long as your heart is geared towards this thing and you don't give up, eventually you will get there. Continue to try, be patient, and believe in yourself and what you're doing. These qualities reaffirm that no matter what didn't work, or what didn't prevail, something eventually will, because you are meant to win. So don't worry about the unknown, just start moving... The road will surely become clearer as you get going.

You may think to yourself, "All of this sounds great, but I still have no control over the fact that I'm afraid or nervous about what can happen. I can't help it." Well, you actually have more control over fear than you think. The most consuming fear usually involves fear of a past hurt repeating itself, or more often than not, fear of the unknown. The first thing you should do when consumed with fear of the unknown is to break the entire scenario down and face it, because it's the things we haven't resolved in our minds yet that make fear so consuming.

When you don't know what to expect, fear is the natural result. Both the unknown and your imagination have no boundaries in your mind, so naturally, neither does the fear you feel. Sometimes, we don't even imagine any specific consequence for something, all we know is that we don't know what to expect, and the result will probably be "bad." If the situation actually happened, however, you would have no choice but to face the entire scenario, figure out a plan and work it through. Often the thing you're so afraid of, when it actually happens it's almost a relief because you're not wondering anymore. Not scared, waiting for the other shoe to drop. Not hiding or avoiding it anymore. So why not just do that now? In any everyday situation that you're running from – bills, a problem at work, a situation you need to discuss or resolve, a truth you must tell, etc. – face the problem.

More than half the time it isn't as bad as you think, and even if it is, knowledge gives you the power to improve the situation. Regardless of what it is, facing it will be the better choice because if you engage the situation, you can open up options. If you avoid it because of fear, whatever it is will happen anyway, and now you have no say in how it happens or affects you. Don't give up your options, even if your decision is to do nothing. Let doing nothing be your choice, not just the way it is. Facing it and having knowledge will always give you a better hand to play, and make whatever it is better to deal with.

For something that has a chance of happening but hasn't actually happened yet, figure out the worst-case scenario and put a plan in place, so if it does happen, you are prepared. You'll find that once you know what you will do if this dreaded thing happened, it doesn't quite have the same hold over you as it did. Don't let fear of things you can't change destroy your life. There are some people so consumed with fear and worry of things that haven't happened or may never happen, that they have subconsciously chosen not to live at all. But it is insane to do this. It is true, there are certain things we cannot control. We just can't. Sometimes we do everything right, yet something seems to go wrong anyway. But all your worrying can't stop it from happening, so choose to live the best life you can. We are often forced in directions that we should have taken ourselves. Then we later learn that this new road was better than we could have ever imagined.

We can't control the future. But we can control how we handle it. Until then, why lose sleep, keep people away and stop facing things because of it? Just LIVE. Whatever is going to happen, is going to happen. Our circumstances do not define who we are. All they are is circumstances. If it happens to you, you can get through it, and if you make up your mind to, there's no doubt you will. Live, and face things as they come. Once you conquer fear, you will feel like you have already won.

Here's the thing with life to remember. As much of a chance that something bad can happen, something good can also happen. Bad does not have a better chance than good, unless you make up your mind that it does and your energy is pulled in that direction. If you find yourself always in a state of fear about bad things happening, then the change needs to start with you. You cannot live your life afraid of what has not even become reality. There are quite honestly too many things to fear, and you will have put your life at a standstill. You are still here, which means that the majority of things you spent time fearing has either never happened, or you survived them. That says a lot about you, and the strength you don't even realize you possess.

Dismiss the negative thoughts and keep moving. You are too busy fighting and winning at the here and now to be trapped in fear because of what "might" happen later. You must continue to fight and win with all you have, even if the odds are against you. Odds have nothing on your will. It doesn't matter how long it takes or how small of a step you take forward; if you keep moving forward, it's still much faster than not moving at all. You will eventually get there, and that is all that matters. Leave uncontrollable circumstances it to your higher power, whether that be the Most High, the Universe, your positive energy, or whatever you believe in.

Here's another thing to consider: your desires and circumstances change, based on what you've achieved today, or where your energy, spirit and heart have walked in the process. The thing you cared about yesterday may not even be important to you or matter by tomorrow. Therefore, concentrate on the now. There are people who don't think good can or will ever happen to them, so they make themselves settle for what they have now. But you have to first be brave enough to reach for something better before you can grab it; if you never reach for it, it will never come.

That's not to say that fighting fear is easy. Maybe something has already happened, like you lost your job, or maybe you're having relationship problems, or maybe you're even having one of the many concerns we experience with our children. But you still have a lot of fight left in you, even if it doesn't feel like it right now. You're still here. That means that you haven't lost yet. This isn't the end. It may be that you fell due to unforeseen circumstances, but you don't have to stay down. The strongest weapon you have against unwanted circumstances is courage. Courage gives you positive energy that grows. Courage gives you strength to take one day at a time, and even more importantly, when it's already happened and the energy of fear has dissipated, the energy of your courage births new ideas, and ideas give you options. Always remember that this is just a circumstance. It is not your life. There are many circumstances. We just have to find the courage to change our present one, and survive until we do. For your children, you must have faith that what you have put into them will shine through. It may take some time, but it took us some time as well at that age. Have faith in who you have raised, or are still raising. Let them make their own mistakes and find their own way. In the end, it is still their life to live, not your own. Let them live it.

You're not alone on this ride. Everyone has fears. Everyone feels anxiety, worry, or self-doubt. It's never an easy thing to put yourself out there for the world to criticize and judge you with a chance of rejection, no matter how talented, successful, or strong you are. Some people are afraid to even want the things they've dream of out loud. Others have fallen into the habit of not asking for too much, since getting anything, no matter how small, is already more than what they expected. But you want to know the only difference between you and someone who has achieved all they want in life? The difference between you and a successful business owner? You and someone you admire? You and anyone you can think of: a star athlete, a celebrity, an icon? The only difference is they dared to go after what they wanted, despite the fear they felt inside. That is ALL. They are human just like you, and feel fear just like you. Fear is a real emotion that we all feel, but once you accept that it can be overcome because people do it every day, you begin to learn how to control it. Then you will already be ahead of the game.

Part of overcoming fear is never being afraid to be you. To venture out and be different, or to tell people how you really feel or who you really are. If they don't accept the real you, then they were never in your corner in the first place. The exception to this is parents – their emotions are fueled by what they want or think is best for their children, and it can cause them to be judgmental or less understanding when they should be allowing their grown children to live their own lives. But never underestimate their love for you and how powerful love can be, despite their feelings on a particular matter. It may just take them some time to see your vision. In the end, you still must be true to you, no matter what they do.

For people in your life who constantly bring you down mentality or spiritually, the thought of your life without them can be scary, but keeping them in your space can also weigh down your spirit, and easily detour you from your goals. These people use hurtful words that discourage you and slowly break your will. You don't have to hate them, even if they're mean or unkind to you. As a matter of fact, you shouldn't. Their actions are because their own spirit is broken, and they may come from a long line of broken spirits. This is a learned behavior, so being unkind may be all they know. It may even be their own fears they're displaying when discouraging you from your dreams. But pitying or understanding them and allowing them into your personal space are two different things. Don't be afraid to let go of these people. Love them from a far if you must. But wish them well and begin to heal from a distance, and your path will begin to look much clearer.

Finally, fight confusion that can cause fear. Confusion in your mind is usually a sign of internal unrest. You feel unsure about your decisions, unsettled and weary. Often this breeds the fear of making the wrong decision, or the fear of rejection. But confusion can be conquered if you understand that there are no "mistakes." You are where you are for a reason, even if you end up simply learning something from it and moving on. Your mistakes are life lessons, and your accomplishments are stepping-stones – therefore everything you do in this life still takes you to another point in your journey.

First, try to find out why you feel so confused. Are you at peace? Is there a lot of turmoil in your life? When you feel internal chaos, you cannot hear when your spirit is speaking. Sometimes the problem is simply a matter of quieting your mind, and changing your perspective. If you are not sure about a decision, the simplest, most powerful thing you can do is wait. When you don't feel secure in what to do and the decision can wait, put it off for a while, until it feels clearer. This allows time for your emotions to settle down and logic to set in, or for your spirit to take over and guide you properly. This also goes for when you want to do something, but something inside just doesn't feel right. Don't ignore this feeling, just wait a while. The right answer almost always presents itself without any further stress.

Your entire life is a big, wonderful journey. Every step you take in it is not your end result, just another step. Therefore, it's okay to not have it all figured out right at this minute. You are always where you are right now for a reason, so move forward without any fear. Evaluate your present situation with a clear, quiet mind that is void of negative energy and stress. Then you can possibly see what your situation can teach you, and how it can aid you in your future goals. Fear is a natural feeling, but pushing past the fear is one of the biggest things you could do to get where you want to go in this world, and feel like you are finally winning. You will never regret facing fear, no matter what the outcome is, because the thing you feared no longer has a hold on you, or your life, ever again.

The Internal Light

Rule Your Destiny.

Do you ever wonder, if humans are so capable of limitless things, why is it that so many of us never fulfill our life's dreams? Henry David Thoreau said, "Most men lead lives of quiet desperation, and go to the grave with the song still in them." Though many of us do reach society's definition of "success" – a good job, a fairly nice home, even marriage, children, etc. – deep inside we know that our own bar of success goes so much deeper than that... if only we would allow ourselves to consider the possibilities. Too many of us instead find ourselves accepting a cycle of mediocrity that never seems to end. It is like dying a grain of salt a day; it's not enough to kill you, but the dull pain of something slowly eating at you never ends.

Whether we are talking about going after a goal or a dream, taking a chance at love, opening your heart to wanting something more for your life, finding peace in your home, or simply having faith in something bigger than yourself – there could be several different reasons why people merely exist in this world, rather than live their best life:

– People are afraid to want something they may never get, and be left disappointed or heartbroken.

– People do not feel themselves deserving of something special or extraordinary.

– People are afraid to actually achieve their dreams, and discover the unknown.

– People would rather accept what they already know, than risk what they presently have for something unfamiliar.

– And finally, and this is a hard one... some people are just not willing to do what it takes to get there.

While most of these reasons appear obvious, there's one point here that seems quite strange. While going after our goals, there's a fear that many of us don't expect. Many call it the fear of success. But that sounds crazy, right? Are we really afraid to win? To essentially get where we've always dreamed of going, or to finally get what we've always wanted? Well, the answer is yes and no. As we get closer to our wants and dreams, when something we never imagined happening actually looks like it's going to become a reality, we begin to feel a fear that we've never experienced. Sometimes it's enough to make a person to turn back. But what we are feeling is not a fear to win. What we are feeling is a fear of the unknown.

When our desires are still dreams – far from our reach and only in our minds – if it doesn't happen, it's okay – it really was only a dream. But when we actually get closer to this dream in our lives, it suddenly transitions in our thoughts from something unattainable, to something that we can actually see or reach. Something that is now close to being real. This transition suddenly brings with it a rush of anxiety: What if something goes wrong? What if your mind is just making you think that you could have this, but you never will? Or what if you actually do reach it, it's the sweetest thing you've ever known, and then it gets ripped from your hands? What if the people in your life will not love you anymore because you've reached one of your dreams, and they may possibly never reach theirs? What if your friends or family will act different towards you now? What if you get there and the reality is not all that you dreamed it would be, essentially killing your idea of this dream?

What all of these scenarios boil down to in your mind is really just one question: What will happen to you now? The idea of success, for many, is an unknown place. Failure or less than ideal situations, are sadly much more familiar. Some people would rather not take a chance to get to success, for fear of all that they do not know. Suddenly what you have right now doesn't seem so bad! In your mind, you think it's not that great, but at least you know what to expect, so it's safe because it can't disappoint you.

But this is what mediocrity looks like. It begins when we convince ourselves that what we have right now is all we should hope for, and whatever it is, we should be grateful for it. No one gets everything they want, because no one's life is perfect, right? So why should you strive for more? It's as if we are never satisfied with what God gave us. Shouldn't we just be grateful and satisfied? This thinking is the biggest lie we've ever told ourselves. First off, being grateful for what you already have has no bearing on reaching for more. You absolutely should be grateful for what you have. But no matter what life you strive for, you will never reach perfection, because we are not perfect creatures, therefore perfection is not within our reach. But when you reach for what your life's purpose is, what desire burns in your heart, what would make you feel light like air, then you don't need perfection. Because that journey you're about to take, that thing you're going to reach for and attain – that is all the perfection you need.

Allowing yourself to want more and then opening your heart to receive it is very scary, because it makes you vulnerable. Vulnerable to what you'll feel if you never reach it. Vulnerable to someone or something crushing this beautiful idea in your head into pieces. Vulnerable to what you might lose in order to find what you want to gain. It takes a great deal of will to push past this fear, because it's one we never expected, so it's a fear we never prepared for. But it is more common than we know, and leaves countless people turning back at the very closest point of winning. You must ask yourself if what you want is worth taking this chance. And here's a hint for you... if it's something you've always wanted, it always is.

Another factor so very disheartening is the people that you love discouraging you, or making you feel guilty for wanting more for your life. Words have power over you, especially the words of the ones you love, and a surprising number of people don't reach for what they want because others have convinced them that their dreams are unrealistic, or made them feel guilty for wanting to go off and be or do more.

The idea of being able to get somewhere that you've dreamed about for so long can feel extremely lonely. You begin to wonder, are you abandoning your family and friends that never made it? Is this wrong? You worry about what will happen. Will they resent you? What will happen to your relationships? Never feel bad to go after what you want. For the people that truly love you will always be by your side. You should only feel bad if you didn't give it your all, or if you were too afraid to take a chance. Everyone's road is not the same. And there's nothing wrong with following your own, even if it's a different course from all those around you.

There are still yet another group of people that sit in situations where they are downright unhappy, yet they won't do anything to change it. There's a level of acceptance, of complacency that people create, yet they don't even realize they're doing it. It happens by them ignoring situations they know in their hearts need to change, but they don't want to face – sort of like throwing a blanket over the problem (in their minds), and covering it up, so it's not as obvious. This avoidance of the truth allows them to live with the problem easier, but by doing that, they've subconsciously accepted it. Do that often enough and before you know it, you're sitting in a life that you do not like, and even though you're not facing it, your spirit still knows the problem is there and is not at peace. So despite all your "ignoring," it still ends up affecting your mood, your relationships – basically your life.

Even worse, if the problem is ever blatantly displayed in front of your eyes – or worse, in front of others – that blanket you placed over those problems will be pulled away from you in a sudden and unforgiving way. Now you have no choice but to face it – only now, it's not on your own terms. And that harsh reality is way more than many of us want to experience, because deep inside, you already know that this is not the life you're supposed to be living. Face your issues, no matter how uncomfortable they are, because no one should be unhappy, even if it is in silence.

So how do we change our lives from a state of wanting, to a state of getting what we want?

People think wanting something badly enough will make you win at achieving your goals. They're quick to say that if you haven't succeeded, you didn't want it bad enough. But who wants to be an addict? Who wants to be overweight? Who wants have a dead-end job, or worse, no job at all? Who wants to fail at their own business venture? What person wants to be left heartbroken and alone, or not feel love? People want things all the time, yet years can pass and they are still in the same place. You must use these wants to fuel your driving force, and use that force to strengthen your mind.

I can't speak enough about your **driving force**. It is a hunger, a deep yearning. It's your feelings, your failures and your truths at the forefront of your mind, where you cannot hide from them, or push them away. It's facing all the things that have prevented you from succeeding in the past. Your driving force is the reason why achieving this goal is so important to you. It's a constant reminder of how this hurdle affects you in your everyday life, and what achieving this goal will do to improve your happiness. It's deciding once and for all that you're willing to do whatever it takes to get there, regardless of all of your past attempts and falls. Your driving force is forever conscious of what you are doing, and always reminds you why you're doing it.

You have to be willing to do what it takes. And doing what it takes cannot be taken lightly, because as we've learned, the mind and heart do not like change. They like routine, and they like what they know. Whether what they know is good or bad is totally irrelevant – as long as it's familiar, your mind and heart are in many ways "comfortable," because they have already learned how to deal with whatever your present situation is.

Even small change is not welcome. Think of something as simple as cooking in someone else's kitchen – it can be done, but it's not a comfortable feeling. Don't underestimate the dedication it takes to fight past familiarity. It is difficult, but not impossible. You can make new habits, and new routines. And as your heart and mind become accustomed to new things, so your body will follow, and your strength will increase.

People often say that as you keep doing difficult things, it gets easier. This statement is untrue and an insult to anyone's hard work. Things do not get easier as you keep doing it, they simply feel easier to you now because you have become stronger. You have the ability to build your mind up to a strength that is stronger than any average person. The more you exercise your mind with your driving force, the stronger it gets. The more you push forward and see results, the stronger the mind gets. The more you accomplish something you've never thought was even possible for you to do, the stronger it gets.

The day you survive your first setback, brush yourself off and realize it can never stop your train from moving forward, the stronger you become. When your mind becomes this strong, you'll know deep inside that there is nothing you won't push past or fight through to get where you're going. When you're tired, your mind pushes past that. When there are no more options, your mind works until it finds one. When it seems like all you've done has failed, your mind is strong enough to simply look at it as a setback, not a failure, and keep going. Never underestimate the goal you are trying to achieve as being easy. If it were easy, you would have done it already. Be prepared for the fight in front of you. Because the fight will surely come. And if you are not prepared, you will fall. Not fail – failing is entirely up to you, because when you fall, you always have the option of getting back up and trying again.

If you keep it up, if you stay strong of mind and will and you don't give up, the universe that you never thought would be in your favor, this world that made you believe this type of happiness just "doesn't happen for you," this life that has beaten you up and made you feel at times that you'd never make it – They all will have no choice but to get out of your way and allow you to get where you're trying to go, because they now know that you won't accept anything less.

What helps you draw this type of energy? Where do you start? Rulers of their own destiny all have similar frames of mind.

There Are No Failures.

Conquerors accept setbacks as just that – falls, stumbles, hurdles, sidetracks; they are only part of their story. The story never ends for a winner until they reach their destination, no matter how many times they fall. Time is not a factor. As long as they keep moving forward, things must, and will, happen for them. It doesn't matter how much you want something, not succeeding in it over and over can be very discouraging. This is where your continued faith and driving force kick in. How much you did the last time doesn't matter – not if it didn't get you where you should be. If you need to put in more, do it. If you need to do it differently, or even change your focus or direction, do it. Pride has no place here, not being able to succeed in the direction you thought you should have doesn't matter. If you failed miserably, publicly, if you lost a great deal of money, it doesn't matter. Winners don't give up, and winners don't stop. You never stop until you win. Remember that this journey you are taking starts now. It's not simply about the end goal. It's about what you learn along the way, how you become strong, how you find your light, your balance, and your love. The key is to accept where you are with humility, being the best in whatever you are doing and wherever you are, while at the same time, believing in your purpose and where you are going, and working towards better. Be the best you can be, no matter what you're doing, learn what you need to from your present experiences, and fill your purpose with working towards something better, while waiting for what comes to you.

Continued Renewal.

Continued renewal is paramount, as we discussed. When you are working towards something, if your mind isn't focused on it constantly, you have already lost. Winning every battle begins with your mind and spirit. So your mind must remain focused and in a positive state, using methods like: Meditation, Spiritual Guidance, Reading, Writing, Quiet Time to Think, Affirmations and Reflection.

These are all the times that your spirit finds the answers that it needs. Are you on the right track? Should you change direction? This is when frustration finally goes away and you find clarity. This is when emotions take a back seat for what the right reactions should be to what is going on around you. This is when you tap into the answers that are not so obvious. Remember while you're going after your dreams and goals, life is still happening: Bills, job, family – chaos that you still have to balance. If you do not have continued renewal for your mind and spirit, then you can lose focus very quickly. You need time for literally just you and the universe.

You and your thoughts, your fears to fight, your dreams to form, and your problems to be thought out. This is the time for you and the God you serve, if it applies. People can give you advice, teach you things and give you information, but this life you are living is still your own. Your life decisions must come from you. If you are not making them, then you are not ready to win.

Your Purpose!

We briefly spoke earlier about purpose. The power and energy that needs to be present in your life in order for success to happen, comes from the purpose that you realize within yourself, then set out to achieve. If you don't have a purpose and are just hoping for the best or think your wants are enough, you will sit around and wonder where all the years have gone and why things haven't happened for you.

You must find your purpose. Everyone in this world has a purpose. A contribution to life. An innate gift that you need to tap into. Find out what that is. It doesn't have to be grandiose, just something that makes you feel complete. The thing that no matter how much you try to leave it alone, your mind and heart just won't let you. The most successful people in this world started with a passion for something, not simply a desire for success or money. Take all of your energy, and focus it into that one thing, then never give up. When you pursue your passion, you will soon find your purpose as well. When we find out what is important and go after these things in life, the money will also come, and often in abundance.

People with purpose don't get beaten up by life. They control the parts of their lives that are controllable, practice humility in the parts they cannot, and make the best of both. If they are not where they want to be, they are not worried, because they are confident that they will get there. And they do, because these types of people are difficult to ignore. No matter how small of a role they may seem to be in at the moment, they are always seen. No situation or role is invisible. Not for someone with a purpose. Never let your present situation dictate your desired one. Your purpose will lead you right to where you need to be.

Make A Plan.

You cannot "hope" to win at something, no matter how big or small. You can't even simply pray to succeed. You must back up your mental thoughts and hopes with physical action. Be intentional in your life. Every goal you want to achieve should begin with preparation. This plan is not meant to be perfect, but what it does is set your wants into motion. You may not always know which road to take to reach your goal, but if you make a plan, you can implement it and move forward.

As you move forward and learn and grow, your plan will evolve over time and become more solid, as you will become more confident with every experience. Don't be afraid to learn what you can to get where you are trying to go. If you don't know, ask questions. Do research. Read. Perform trial and error. Experiment. Some people have a want, and it stops there. Don't just sit around and be unhappy that things aren't happening for you. Take as much control over your life as you possibly can. Even in bad situations. Uncomfortable ones. Ones that you feel you can't control. You can always control something, even if it's just your feelings or your reactions. And as long as you are alive and have breath in your body, you still have an opportunity for things to change.

Find Your Faith.

Success is not for the faint-hearted. It takes work, focus, patience and determination. But to be truly successful, you must have one more thing that keeps you strong until you reach your goal, and that's faith. Faith is what allows you to see what is not yet physically visible. You may be the only one that sees it, but you are the only one that matters. The others will come around. Remember, there were no computers before someone invented them. Or houses. Or electricity. Or highways. Or even straws. They all started in someone's mind, and came alive through their faith. If your mind can see it, then you can make it so. Until then, let your faith keep you going when everyone else thinks you should give up. Let it keep you investing in yourself, when everyone thinks it's a waste of time. Let it keep you believing, even when everything in your path indicates that you shouldn't. Success is not the smooth, upward road that people like to paint it to be, no matter how great or solid your dream is. It's full of ditches, corners, detours, valleys and nasty potholes. It takes a great deal of faith, will, and strength to pick yourself up after every fall. As long as you can see it through your faith, you can make it happen.

Prepare For The Storm.

The world is full of chaos, and as soon as you find purpose and get moving, it seems like problems just appear out of nowhere. Circumstances that were never there before are suddenly emerging. Why is it that when you are finally trying to go after something, all these bad things start happening to you? It feels like you can never win, or worse, you were never meant to. But you are not meant to fail, and there isn't anything happening to you that hasn't happened to everyone else who pursued more for their lives.

As difficult as these roadblocks can be, many who've traveled that road before have learned not to look at these circumstances as a bad thing; rather, they look at them as an indication that they are on the right track, because difficulty always seems to appear right before you get to the finish line. Difficulty is here to first test, then strengthen your resolve. It's almost as if its intention is to ask, "Do you really want this?" Not just in your mind, but in your heart.

Success is not unreachable for anyone. But it is the road less traveled, because it is difficult. If you really want this – more than you're afraid, more than you want your comfort, more than whatever difficult circumstance comes your way – push past it all, become stronger, and the difficulty will eventually go as easily as it came. So when you feel like giving up, that's the time to push harder, because success is almost always about a half-mile past the point of wanting to give up. If you just keep going, then you'll finally be able to turn that corner.

Now that we've gone through the things you should gravitate towards and implement in your life in order to succeed, you should also be aware of the things you should do away with and push away from. Just as powerful as your mind is when positive energy is present, it can be just as damaging when you let negative elements in. Besides fear, guilt, doubt and confusion that we discussed, there are other negative elements to look out for. Some are outside elements, others are right here at home.

Procrastination Is The Thief Of Time.

Procrastination is quite stealthy. If you give it power, it will leave you with nothing achieved. Nothing to smile about. Nothing to be proud of. The worst thing about procrastination is it has way more power than we give it credit for. We could be procrastinating for literally years. Did we start out thinking it would be that long? Absolutely not! We'll start next week. We'll start after our vacation. We'll start when the kids get out of school. We'll start when we have more money. But regrettably, the ideal time never came, and often we don't even realize what's happening until it's too late.

Have you ever by chance, while spring cleaning maybe, found some goals you'd written down... weeks, months, or even years ago? "Be out of debt by December." "Lose 20 pounds by September 1st." "Move out, get my own place by January 15th." Here it is two years later, and you haven't even lost the first 5lbs, or paid off the first debt. Next thing you know, years have gone by. And we could have achieved what it was we wanted to years ago, if we had just given it the small amount of time it needed. What causes procrastination? Well, procrastination often involves one of three things: thinking we have time, thinking we're not ready, and anxiety. All are silent, but deadly killers. The first: time. We always think we have time. But while we're waiting because we think our time is infinite, time is steady moving. Not waiting on anyone or anything. That's how weeks, months and years go by, and we don't know where it went. We don't have all the time in the world. And all the time you're wasting is time you could have achieved something and been happier in your life. Stop wasting time. You don't know how much of it you have left, and every day you don't do something is another day you're still unhappy. Just get started.

The second: We think we're not ready. "I want to start this business, but I don't really have the money." "I want to redo my house, but I'm going to wait until the kids are gone." "I want to save money, but I barely have enough to get by, so I can't save much." So we wait until the perfect time, and the perfect time never comes. And it never will come, because there is no such thing. If you want to do something, just do it. There is no such thing as too "little" or not enough when it comes to making a change, because change happens from consistency, which builds momentum.

If you only have 20 minutes in the morning to work out, use it. Change will happen slowly, but surely. It's better than working out for two hours one day, then not going back. Don't be discouraged by how little you can save, or what someone else is saving. If you could only save $20 every paycheck, it doesn't matter, start saving. In time, it will add up. And it will mean something. Eventually you'll be able to save more. And in a few years, you'll know you made the right decision. Even small steps eventually get you where you're trying to go, and almost always, when you start building momentum, you'll find that things start happening a lot quicker than you imagined.

Anxiety.

We imagine what we will have to go through to get where we want to go, or what will happen if we face that problem. We want to do it, we may even know that we need to do it. But we surely aren't looking forward to whatever we think we might have to do to get there. So we put it off. And put it off. And time just passes by. The funny thing about all this is it's almost always worse in your head than it actually is. We procrastinate and avoid even the smallest things: That call you're dreading. That letter that keeps coming in the mail. That conversation you need to have with your son. Whatever your motivation for procrastination is, demolish it.

Start that workout regimen, even if it's Thursday. Who says we need to start something in the beginning of the week or month, or January 1st? Don't avoid the unknown. Have that conversation with your mother, or husband, or friend that you've been avoiding. When you stifle your needs, you stifle your growth. If you need something from someone, whether it's support, affection, understanding or even forgiveness, you won't feel whole until you go after it. Even if you don't get it, the only thing you'll ever regret is never trying. The rest is on them, not you.

Start that business. You won't feel completely happy until you try. Make up with that person that you love. Life is too short to give pride that much time over it. Finally, when you're feeling lazy (we all do sometimes), think of what this little sacrifice now, will mean for your goals later. This small investment will have a huge payoff, and it is always worth it.

Demolishing procrastination from your life will always leave you leading a richer, fuller, happier life.

Negative people.

Negative people are powerful killers of dreams. We are so much more lenient with negative people than we should be. People that complain ALL the time. People that never have something positive, encouraging, loving, or supportive to say. They drain your energy with their drama and complaining. Then you unwittingly share your most precious dreams with them, and they make you feel like the craziest person alive. Why on earth do we do this? Because they are old friends. Because they have no one else. Because he/she is just going through something right now, as always. Excuses. You only have one life. ONE. Never feel bad to rid your life of people that bring nothing but negativity to drain you of happiness. Do not apologize for keeping your life stress and negative-free. Because negative energy travels. It gets into your spirit and drains the mind, as well as the soul. Rid yourself of them. You'll be lighter, freer, and better off.

Coveting.

What a negative thing to allow into your mind. There are some people that measure their degree of success or failures with someone else's. What someone else has achieved, what someone else's body looks like, how long it took this person to accomplish something, how much money they have, what car they drive, if they're married already, etc.

You cannot measure your success based on someone else's because they are not you. Your potential, your drive, your talent, your wants and your determination are your own. They need to live their best life, and you need to live yours. It is the reason why there is no blueprint for an amazing life because my idea of amazing is not yours, and your idea of it is not the next guy's. Neither is better, they are all just uniquely created in each person's mind to give them their own happy. So if you're going after someone else's happy, you're actually moving further away from yours. And the sooner you realize that, the better off you will be.

One of the biggest reasons why coveting is a bad idea is if you use someone else's barometer of success instead of your own, you could be limiting your own potential. If it's more important for you to know how someone else did just to make sure you've beaten them, then you're not living up what your best really is. Maybe their best is a C and yours is an A+. But you'll never know that if you got a B and you're using them as your bar of achievement. Maybe they were only supposed to go this far in a particular career and move on, but you were supposed to go much further, yet you've lost focus because they've changed paths. The journey you have to take is your own, and it can be amazing if you'd only stop trying take someone else's.

Second reason this is a bad idea is you don't know what someone had to do to get where they are. You don't know what someone had to give up or sacrifice to live the life their living, and maybe the price is more than you are willing to pay. You don't know how many nights someone stayed up after work to get that degree so they could make more money and have that beautiful home. You don't know how many no's that person heard before they got the right yes. You can't possibly expect to be where someone is if you have not walked in their shoes. Use them as encouragement, not a point of envy. You have your own goals, your own speed and your own pace.

On the other side of that coin, you don't know who a person stole from to now walk around as if he's earned something you're still working towards. Maybe someone is spending money like rain, but living off of someone else. Just because everything looks good on the outside doesn't mean it is so. You could stay envying a girl's relationship wondering why yours isn't that way, not knowing she gets abused or cheated on. You could wonder why the guy next door looks so successful while you're still struggling, not knowing he is drowning in debt and about to lose his house. You could wonder how someone was able to pass a test you studied so hard for and he made it seem so easy, not knowing this is the third time he's taken this exam.

The only person that truly knows a person's life is that person. You have to set your standards based on YOU. Your life up to this point, plus your intentions, desires and goals of happiness is what will dictate your journey. Accept where you are, and look forward to where you are going. Your destiny is your own, and you can't possibly see how far you've come or how much you've achieved, if all you're doing is wishing you had someone else's life. You'll never have their life. So love yours – for all it is, all it isn't, and all it can be.

Success seems like the longest road to travel. But in this life, you must remember, you can only fail if you quit trying. And once you start your journey towards a better life and continue to reach for more, you'll soon learn that part of the happiness you're seeking, is already coming into fruition.

Sharing Your Walk in Life.

Relationships. Complicated, sometimes painful, yet so necessary in our lives. As with most things in life, many of us spend an excessive amount of time chasing something that was in us all along. This book was meant to uplift, renew and help you discover the greatness you have inside of you. But to ignore the need that we feel to have companionship, someone to share our life and happiness with, it would then not fully encompass all aspects of one's happiness.

If you remember nothing else in this chapter, remember this: There is a direct connection between the manner in which you love yourself and how you will end up loving someone else, as well as how someone will be inclined to love you back. Relationships – whether romantic, platonic, business or family – are always directly affected by the health of your own internal state. This is why repairing yourself first is so very important. It is a necessary foundation needed to build and maintain healthy relationships, yet it's the one step that many people disregard; instead, they look for the relationship or loved one to repair what's broken inside of them, or fill the emptiness they feel. That is also why this chapter is at the end of the book instead of the beginning; you should already be past the stage of feeling lost or broken before looking to share your life with someone else.

What is now in you is what you have to give to a relationship. If you have nothing, the relationship will have no substance. If you have turmoil, the relationship will also be in turmoil. Similarly if you have love, you can give your relationship love; if you have promise, you can give your relationship promise, and so this rule applies to all elements of a relationship. If you are already in a relationship, all is not lost – still concentrate on repairing yourself from within and the rest will come, whether it is to stay and work on something worth repairing, or to leave because it is no longer in keeping with your expectations.

Simply caring for someone, no matter how deeply, is not all that it takes to have a healthy relationship. Furthermore, turmoil that isn't resolved within you from the past doesn't just dissipate; it lives indefinitely, seeping into your new relationship, and possibly even getting passed on to your children. So if you truly love someone, work on repairing yourself so your love isn't burdened with hurt, anger, pain, and resentment – and instead, can be transcended into love that is light, open, giving, and nurturing – adding to your happiness.

The most valuable thing we could do when looking for a partner or a healthy relationship is to change our way of thinking. Many discuss alarming divorce rates as a reason to not get married. But not enough people discuss how many of those relationships could have been saved if they had better communication, respect or understanding. The unity of marriage is not the problem, usually it is our expectations of marriage that are unrealistic, while not spending enough time giving the relationship what it actually needs to be loving, giving, and nurturing.

We think of marriage as always fun. Always happy. Always romantic. But marriage is a part of life, and life will always have ups and downs. The same way we shouldn't give up on life, we shouldn't be so quick to give up on marriage. Surprisingly, infidelity is not the leading cause of divorce. Leading causes include: finances, codependency, unmet expectations, and more often than not, simply an inability to resolve conflicts. These all boil down to a lack of three things: communication, respect and personal responsibility. Work hard on these things and find the root of the destructive behavior in your relationship, so it you can rid your home of it, and your relationship can become stronger and lasting.

Know first that other relationships are not this one. If you are not ready to give this person what they deserve, then don't waste their time. You would not want your mate's old

of you. And before you say it, no, they should not be understanding of your past hurt as an excuse to mistreat them
(and neither should you, if the roles are reversed). For instance, your past relationship is not an acceptable reason
for your extreme mistrust if they gave you no reason to feel
that way, just because someone in your past did. It also it
not a good reason for you to be quick to anger because
someone in the past always wanted to fight with you.

Past relationships should never be your reason to not be
giving or fair in a new one, just because someone who is no
longer here abused your kindness in the past. If you are not
healed, then you should leave this new person alone and
let them find someone who is going to treat them with the
love, trust and respect they deserve. No one deserves to be
punished for the actions of another person. It is unfair, and
unkind. Yet so many people think it's okay to get involved
with someone and treat them badly because of the pain
someone else caused. You're not healed, but you're lonely.
So you venture out and get involved with someone, knowing you only have half of a heart to give. It is a selfish thing
that people casually do all the time. Your pain is perfectly
normal. Taking time to get over it is equally just as normal
– and necessary. Take your time and heal. We will always
have things we need to work on. But we should at least wait
until we are strong enough and healed from the past before
starting a new relationship, and passing the hurt someone
gave you to someone else.

Let the Fantasy Go.

Most of us have this idea of the perfect partner: a certain height, certain weight, certain financial status, certain personality. We have it all figured out, until we realize we don't. Happiness can take place in your life, even if it doesn't look the way you expected it to. Don't put unreasonable restrictions on finding a mate. We all have preferences, but the potential of a wonderful mate is not restricted to a couple of inches in height, or a number on a scale. You can miss out on a completely wonderful person with such strict requirements. The best thing you can do is accept that no one has to be perfect, in order to be amazing.

Love Yourself First.

Before you go out there looking for love, make sure that you love yourself first. Before seeking to share your life with someone else, be conscious of how you feel about yourself... Do you love who you are? Do you truly believe that you are deserving of someone good? If you do not, then you should not be looking for someone to love and for you to trust at this time. Because no matter how much you want to love someone, if deep inside you do not love yourself or believe you deserve something or someone good, you will not make good decisions, nor will you be able to recognize when someone good has actually come along.

You must first feel love for yourself before you can truly love someone else without fear. Low self-esteem and love do not make a good pair. When you are broken, you tend to gravitate towards others who are broken. When you love yourself, you tend to have standards. Looking for a person who will love you is not enough. A person can have the worst standards, morals and behaviors in the world, and can still love you. People who have low self-esteem can love you, too. But if they don't love themselves, they can never love you in the way you need to be loved. So when looking for a partner, love is not enough. When you are whole, you can recognize relationships that are selfish and unkind, and you will be strong enough to rid yourself of them, or avoid them altogether. When you love yourself, you can also fight insecurities with a much stronger hand. Insecurity can rear its ugly head in any relationship, no matter how strong you are. Always know that there will always be someone that has more of something – whether it's money, attractiveness or even fancy words – but it never means they can replace you. There is only one YOU. That is why your partner chose you. Not because you were the best at anything. They chose you simply because you are the best person for them.

Be an Individual.

When in a relationship, remember to also live a full life. Your relationship should enhance your life, not be your life. You should not base your entire happiness on your partner, and similarly, you should not expect them to do the same. This is the definition of an unhealthy relationship. It puts too

132

much pressure on your relationship and can lead to disaster. A healthy relationship is one that consists of two happy, healthy individuals that come together and create something great. Being great together doesn't mean that they aren't whole individually; it just means that each part of this synergy is valuable in its own way, so when they come together, it's amazing. You should already know who you are, and where you are going. You should know what you like and have your own friends. You should have your own hobbies and your own interests. You should have a vision for your future, even if that vision changes slightly when you get together. As a couple, you will share interests as well as discover new things and find hobbies together, but having your own life is still important. Never give up all of what you love and have a passion for when getting into a relationship. Never leave all your friends behind and be upset when your partner wants to be with their own friends. We were not meant to be codependent on each other. We were meant to enhance each other's lives, complement each other, and add something beautiful to one another.

Reciprocity.

Give as much as you want in return. A surefire way to head for disappointment is to look for someone to give you a great deal of what you want, while you are not as willing to give back as much in return. Everyone has feelings, and we all have our own wants and needs. You cannot expect someone to give you everything you want, while you disregard everything that they want. You may not see their needs as important, but just as you want that person to care enough about you to want to make you happy, you need to do the same. Your needs don't have to be the same or even similar, you just need to both have the same willingness to fulfill them. When you know your worth, you are not afraid to express what you need, and you're more likely to know the value of respecting someone else's needs as well. This is why being whole is so important, because it makes you a better partner. Always remember to pay attention to your partner's wants. You have no idea how much it means when you do something or make a gesture, regardless of how small, solely to make the person you love happy.

Compromise.

We all know this one, but we don't like to do it – you must compromise. Many people think telling them to compromise is telling them to settle, but it is simply not true. There is a distinct difference between compromising and settling. Compromise is paramount to a healthy relationship. Let's just think about what relationships are for a moment: Two different people, with two different minds, different wants and different needs, coming together to form one bond, and make one future together. There must be compromise in that equation, so that both parties get things that they want, and things that make them happy. That is part of giving as much as you want to receive.

But what is the difference between settling and compromise? Remember that if it is something you want or would like in your life, it is something you can compromise on. If it is something that you need and will not be happy without it, or your well-being will be compromised, then living without it is settling. A woman might like a guy that is 6'2", but she doesn't need it. A guy may want a woman that has long legs, but he won't need it. Someone, however, may need to be with someone who shares his or her religious beliefs. Someone else may need to be with someone who shares their wants for children, or their outgoing spirit. And we all need someone who will love us with honesty and respect.

There is no blueprint, because everyone's needs are different. In order to go after what you truly need, you must first have knowledge of SELF; thoroughly examining who you are with no apologies, then fearlessly going after what you know you need to make you happy. But in a relationship, you will not always get what you want. This is part of the give and take, and this person's needs are just as important as yours, so make sure you commit to someone who you love enough to want to make them happy. Making your husband or wife happy should actually bring you some joy as well. In that same spirit of compromise, remember that every disagreement is not worth winning, and every argument is not worth the end result. Sometimes when we are upset, we lose sight of what's important. But words are something we can never take back, and they can truly be the turning point in a relationship. So be mindful of what you say to the person you love. There are many forms of compromise in a relationship, and they can all at some point make you feel like you are losing something. But if you think about it, everything in life consists of give and take. Is what you're getting worth what you are giving? It should be. If it is not, then you need to reevaluate your relationship. But if this is the right relationship and the person you truly love and want is by your side, chances are, it is very much worth it. Compromise, and live a happier life with the person you love.

Find Respect Again.

Respect is a key ingredient that needs to be present in any successful, happy relationship. You need to insist on getting respect, as well as you need to give it. Many don't think of respect as an area where improvement needs to take place, because they reason that they don't experience disrespect. After all, they don't encounter abuse, rudeness, being talked down to, cursing, cheating, and so on, from their significant other. But these are simply the more common, blatant examples of disrespect.

What about when you don't respect your spouse's feelings? What if you don't respect their opinion, or his/her voice? What if you override what your husband says to the children, so the children don't feel the need to respect his authority? What if you've been ignoring something your wife has been telling you for years that she cannot stand to deal with? What if you don't respect each other as individuals, or respect each other's dreams, passions or interests?

There are many aspects to this thing called respect, and they are all important to a healthy partnership. Respect is directly related to many other significant attributes: regard, consideration, honor, appreciation, etc. You don't have to be 'disrespectful' in the common sense of the word to lack respect for your partner in a relationship. Furthermore, the way your significant other displays respect for you will also have a huge impact on how others respect you: family, the children, even friends. And that level of respect, or lack thereof, can greatly affect your peace.

Respect must be reciprocal in order for it to be whole. Just as you expect it, you must be conscious of giving it consistently. In a relationship, respect is not gender-specific. Both men and women need respect and consideration, and not receiving it causes other aspects of the relationship to fall out of balance.

But lack of respect isn't always so black and white. There isn't always a bad guy, or someone being malicious or intentionally hurtful. Lack of respect could be because you don't realize how you are making your partner feel. It could be because you've never experienced an equal partnership, and don't know how to be in one. It could even be because of fear.

Let's take the following example. Maria is a single woman. After some bad breakups and periods of loneliness, she eventually learned to adapt to what she feels life has handed her, and since a man was not present, she removed her practical need for him. She had to fend for herself financially, so she did. She had to be a single parent, so she did, and so on. But this adjusted life is not without consequences and scars. Maria may no longer feel a practical need for a man, but love is not practical, so no matter how much she cares for herself, is a great single parent or manages well financially, she still feels the need for love and companionship. So eventually, Maria ventures out and meets Phil, and after some time, she and Phil decide to build a life together.

Now Phil knows she's been hurt before, but he doesn't yet realize that Maria's scars go so much deeper than a bad breakup. In Maria's eyes, she is letting Phil into her already set-up life. It's a life that she is subconsciously very protective of, and although she very much wants his companionship and even welcomes his assistance in a lot of areas, there's a great deal of difficulty for her to treat him as an equal partner when it comes to parenting, finances, their way of living, and other key decisions in their lives. Though not rude or blatantly disrespectful, it is clear to Phil that she does not value his opinion: she doesn't consult with him before making decisions that will affect him as well, she intervenes when he speaks to her children. She doesn't discuss major purchases with him. She allows family members to stay with them without even consulting with him; the list goes on and on. Although she doesn't say it, she really doesn't feel like she needs to talk to Phil for these things. After all, she was taking care of herself before him, right? But this type of controlling behavior is usually rooted in the person's own fear. What if she does make him an equal partner with an equal say and Phil leaves, causing chaos again? Her life has already taught her she cannot rely on anyone. What if he hurts her children, emotionally or otherwise? What if something else goes wrong? Although she loves him, the bottom line is she doesn't want to allow herself to need him.

Is Maria a bad person for being afraid and not wanting to put herself in a position to be hurt? Is Phil a bad person for wanting an equal say in their relationship? Neither is the case. Yet, this situation is a breeding ground for turmoil. What happens next can be a few things. The most common two are that they can argue a great deal and Phil can fight for an equal say in their home, or Phil can just give Maria her way and not say anything, while suppressing feelings of inferiority. Either situation can be the catalyst for a host of bad things to come.

No matter what someone has been through, it is important to understand two things: First, in order to be in a real relationship, you must be willing to be vulnerable. There's no other way that a real relationship will work and there's no go-around. You must put yourself out there in order to reap the reward. Like everything else worth having, you must take a chance. Fear or bad experiences is no excuse for shutting someone out that loves you, or keeping them at a certain distance. We all have fear, and your partner is just as important as you are in this relationship, and taking just as much of a chance. Second, everyone wants to feel like they matter in a relationship. They want to feel like their voice matters, as well as their feelings and their happiness. You are not the only one in this relationship. Therefore, you must give your partner the respect they deserve, and there must be a balance of what both of you want in the life you build together, or the relationship will be destined to fail.

Respect has to be proven in your actions, you can't just say I respect you. You cannot disregard your partner's feelings and still say you respect them. If you are not being treated with the basic respect you deserve and give to your partner, you must love yourself enough to demand it or let go of the relationship altogether. It is simple logic, but not so simple to put into practice. However if you don't, you'll never be happy. Deep inside, the reality of your situation will always be there, and you cannot run from your thoughts, your heart, or your spirit.

When it comes to blatant disrespect, some make excuses for the person treating them badly, saying they are simply rough around the edges, or this is just "how they are" and "they don't mean any harm." But no one should have to put up with feelings of disregard or disrespect from anyone who can help it. Seek respect in every relationship you have, including the one with yourself.

Also remember that treating someone with consideration and high regard is contagious. You'd be surprised how much a person's attitude can change once they notice the manner in which you consistently treat them. This may be a type of love that no one has ever shown them before, and people tend to gravitate towards positivity and will work hard to keep it, because they do not want it to change.

Once you experience a relationship that is based on mutual respect and consideration for one another, it is difficult to go back to anything less. Strive for this in every relationship you have, and preserve your dignity, your self-respect, and your happiness.

Learn… To… Communicate.

Too often, relationships become broken over unspoken feelings. Feelings that could (and should) have been expressed, worked on and resolved. Don't assume that someone should know what you want or what you are thinking. If you want something, simply ask for it. If your partner hurt you, tell them. You should never harbor bad feelings over things that could have been resolved if you'd simply opened your mouth and shared your feelings. Many of us are guilty of this. We stay quiet on the outside, but inside we are fuming, upset and hurt. Meanwhile the person has no idea what is going on.

We need to learn that we are all individuals. We cannot expect people to read our minds, even the ones we love. The worst is saying nothing is wrong when something is most definitely wrong. What do we expect the person to do once you say nothing is wrong? How silly is it that if they don't continue to probe after you said nothing is wrong, you get upset. It's quite senseless the things that we deem to be normal behavior, when so much conflict could be resolved if we'd just expressed how we feel. It's not worth your pain. At least give the person you love the opportunity to fix what's wrong. One can't fix what they're not even aware of.

Persevere, Persist, Endure.

Finally, we must persevere. Many relationships, though not presently in a state of harmony or in sync, are definitely worth saving. The foundation is pure, it's full of love, and full of promise. If you want to stay, what can you do to repair the problem at hand? All that most people think of when their relationships are in turmoil is what the other person is doing, or should be doing. But the reality is the only person in this life we can control is ourselves. So if you truly feel your relationship is worth saving, take steps to see how you can make it better. Stop harping on their part in the problem, and look at yourself. See the part you played, and find out what you can do to change it. Only then can change begin. It seems so hard, but you are already here in the relationship. You are already unhappy. You have nothing to lose by trying, and everything to gain by succeeding. Everyone seems to be waiting for the other person to do something first. But this type of standoff is a waste of energy and precious time, and it is useless. It does nothing but keep you in a place of unhappiness.

Taking responsibility for your part is not saying all the blame is on you. It is being grown-up enough to look at your part in where things went wrong, and take ownership. Doing something as simple as starting the healing by assuming your responsibility and taking action releases positive energy into the situation. And that energy is powerful, as well as transferrable. You would be surprised at how much you changing for the better could effect change in someone else. Your partner may not want to acknowledge it at first, but they will definitely notice your changes. It may even take some time for them to feel like the change is here to stay and not temporary, but after significant time passes, you would have accomplished the most powerful thing you could do; you put the ball in their court. You have eliminated their excuses. You have done away with the things they complained about as the reason for their own negative actions, and now they have no choice but to look at themselves.

After that happens, if they still do not make changes, then guess what? You now know deep in your heart that you have truly done all you can to effect change. You worked at your relationship, and you gave it the chance it deserved. And you will be able to decide with no guilt if it is worth staying in this relationship, or possibly moving on with your life.

If you don't know where to begin to affect change, think to yourself... if this person were giving you everything you needed and was making you happy, what would you do for them? Have 2-5 things come to your mind? Then you know exactly what this person wants or needs from you. It's not as difficult as it seems, once the burden of blame is out of the equation. We know our mate's wants and needs more than we care to admit, and we know what they'd like to see in us, or what would make them happy.

Relationships are almost never as complicated as they seem. What we're supposed to do is just not always what we are willing to do. But nothing worth having is without hard work, patience, and sacrifice. If you're willing to put in the work, the happiness in your relationship will come, or you will find the courage to let go and seek someone who shares your needs for a loving, strong, committed partnership. Either way, the work you put into your relationship will put you well on your way to a happier life, as well as a more meaningful existence.

You are Free.

The Internal Light

Trust Your Journey.

Have you ever noticed that it always seems to take longer to drive somewhere you've never been to before, than it is to return back, the same distance, to your original destination? You may have gotten a little lost along the way going there, but for the most part, the reason it feels longer is that we didn't know where we were going. Reality hardly ever looks like our expectations. We basically just want to get there! Many lose patience on the way there and turn back, when all they had to do was drive just a little longer, and they would have arrived. But just that one trip going there taught us many things, so returning back home never feels as long as the journey there, because we now know what to expect, how long it takes, and where to make our turns.

The thing is, it may feel sometimes like what we are doing is wasting time because we are not seeing our desired result, but if we never kept driving and always turned back, we'd never get anywhere. Map technology has taken some of the guesswork out of driving, but unfortunately we don't have the same technology for our goals and dreams. So many people, more than we'd like to imagine, come so very close to living out their goals and dreams, but 'turn back' or give up prematurely because in their minds, it's not going the way that they expected, or it's not happening as fast as they thought it should. They feel like there just shouldn't be this many turns, or roadblocks, or U-turns. So they simply give up, go back to not trying, and never get there.

In order to get where you are going, besides working hard, being consistent and believing in yourself, you must also trust your journey. If you don't, you may be on the right road, but quit before you get there because it's not happening fast enough, or even in the manner you think it should happen. What does it really mean to trust your journey? Trusting your journey rests on three important things: Patience, Persistence and Faith.

How can you control Patience? When you want something so badly, it is very difficult to be patient. You feel like you can't even help it. But when you exercise Patience, all you are doing is making a decision to accept that there are things in your life you cannot control or change – like time and circumstance – and believe that you will eventually get where you're going, no matter how long it takes or what comes your way. Results never seem to come as fast as we would like it to. But the timing does not determine our success; whatever is meant for you is meant for you, and you will receive it. Remember that you are going down a road you've never been on before, so you can't possibly know all it takes to get there. In fact, not getting there in the time you anticipated should be expected. You may have feelings of failure because you're not yet there, but know that as long as you stay persistent and have faith, there is no such thing as failure. Every step you take, every job you get, every role you play or circumstance you overcome is part of your journey. There is something to learn, an event to take place, someone you must meet or something that must happen before you can get to your destination. Your faith in who you are helps you to remember that you will get there, no matter how long it takes.

But what do you do when your emotions are involved? When you care so much about something or someone, but it just is not happening after "all this time"? How do you leave it alone without being negative, constantly hurt or resentful? In those cases, you should release it to your Higher Power. You are not giving up or becoming resentful, but if you continue to think about it or dwell on it, it only causes you pain. So rather than completely letting it go, you're simply releasing it, so that your Higher Power can take over. Just remember that you are still here, and you haven't been brought this far to fail now. So if it has been decided it is not for you, then it's because it was not the right thing for you. If it is for you, then it will happen when it is the right time.

We of course think the right time is now! We may even think the right time was months ago, even years ago. But there are things that we simply cannot see in the present moment. Things that may need to happen first. Things we need to learn. People that need to leave – or come – before something should take place. There may be some growing that you have to do. And we don't know what even better thing is waiting for us around the corner if this isn't for us. So when you reach that breaking point beyond your control, don't give up. Just let it go, and wait for what comes next. Walk away and keep your faith, because the positive energy you give off about the situation still lends itself to the dream at hand. Be humble, be accepting of the light within you, and be trusting. In the meantime, work on you, so when it or something even better happens, you will be a little more ready than you are now.

You may not be able to control when things happen in your life, but the things you can control are your faith, and your persistence. So first maintain faith in yourself that you will get where you are going, stay positive, and live in the now. When you stay positive no matter what, you are actually still providing energy to the very thing you are waiting for, so you are not powerless. Patience may not be easy at first, but once you master it, you'll find that you never have to wait as long as you think.

Remember, when living out your journey, you have to drive without any navigation. Learn what you can about the journey you're starting, jump in despite your fears and get going, stay focused, get back on track when you find yourself lost, and most importantly, have faith, knowing that eventually, you WILL get there.

Your internal light will guide your way, no matter how dark the road ahead may seem. Just remember that no matter what the problem, dream or desire in your heart is, happiness and peace must always come from you.

###

The Internal Light:
Finding Peace in a World Full of Chaos

www.ingramcontent.com/pod-product-compliance
Lightning Source LLC
Chambersburg PA
CBHW030835090426
42737CB00009B/985